MEN OF THE SHEPHERD

A 100-Day Devotional for Faith, Family, and Leadership

Christopher A. Smith

Empowering Men in Faith and Family First

Published by:

Harvest Field Publishing

Printed in the United States of America

ISBN: 979-8-9951728-2-6

To my son, Christopher,

and my daughter, Angelina

In response to Jesus' call,

and because of you,

this book was written.

Introduction

This book was not written in comfort. It came out of a season of tension, uncertainty, and correction.

In late 2024, I believed God was calling me into missionary work in Thailand. I moved toward it quickly, ready to sell my home and step into what I believed was obedience. Over time, it became clear that I was moving ahead of God, trying to force His timing into mine. What felt like clarity turned into conviction. What I thought was direction became correction. That realization did not come quickly or easily.

Through counsel, prayer, and some hard moments of honesty, I had to slow down and look at something deeper, not just where I was going, but how I was leading my life. Around that same time, I was presented with an opportunity to step into a senior pastoral role, something I was not pursuing, but one that forced me to reconsider everything. At the same time, my children were stepping into their own transitions. My son was moving toward marriage. My daughter was beginning to look ahead. I had to face a simple truth. My role as a father was changing, but it was not ending. My presence still mattered.

This devotional grew out of a YouTube and blog project I began in early 2025. Over several months, I worked through these reflections in real time, not as theory, but as lived experience. Now in 2026, looking back on that season, I felt a clear call to bring it together into this devotional.

This is a call back to that foundation.

Men, your first church is your family, and your first ministry is your home. Never forget that. It is where you will lead with truth and conviction under Christ, with the discipline to stay grounded and the humility to be corrected.

Men, take up the responsibility you have been given. Pick up your sword, the Word of truth (Ephesians 6:17). Stand firm. Lead your family as a Shepherd under Christ. Lead your family as a man of the Shepherd.

With peace and blessings as you carry your sword,

Chris

Day 1

Man of Valor: Leading with Strength and Humility

Judges 6:12 (ESV)
"The LORD is with you, O mighty man of valor."

There was a time when I was convinced I was doing exactly what God wanted. I had set my sights on the mission field, done the research, asked for advice, and made my plans. It all looked right on the outside. But deep down, I never stopped to ask the one question that mattered: Is this truly what God has called me to? I was moving forward with confidence, but it wasn't grounded in obedience. It was driven by something else I didn't want to see.

What I thought was zeal for God was actually pride. I wanted to serve, but I also wanted to be seen as someone who served. Like the sons of Thunder, I had passion without wisdom. When God shut the door, it hit hard. The disappointment wasn't just about a missed opportunity, it exposed something deeper. I realized I had pushed my own will ahead of His. That realization brought a weight I couldn't ignore. I had not just misstepped, I had missed Him.

That was the turning point. I had to face the truth that I was trying to serve God on my terms. I had convinced myself my plans were holy, but they were self-serving. I had overlooked the calling already in front of me. God didn't need my ambition, He wanted my surrender. When I finally humbled myself and let go, clarity came. Peace followed. Not because I got what I wanted, but because I was finally aligned with Him.

God calls men of valor before we see it ourselves. Gideon was hiding, Moses doubted, Jeremiah resisted, but God still called them. The same is true for me, and it's true for you. Strength is not standing alone or forcing your path forward. Strength is standing with God, submitted, led, and dependent on Him. The real calling isn't somewhere out there, it's right here. To shepherd your family, to lead with both strength and humility, and to walk in obedience.

Shepherding Value

Humility in Leadership — Leading your family begins with surrendering pride and following God's direction as a husband and father.

Reflect

1. Jesus calls you to follow His will, not your own—where are you resisting His direction in your relationship with Him?

2. Pride can mask itself as passion—where is your heart pushing ahead instead of submitting to God?

3. Your family depends on your leadership—how can you realign your role as a husband or father with God's calling today?

Live It Today

Pause today and ask God directly where you are leading yourself instead of following Him, then take one step of obedience in your home.

Personal Prayer

Lord, expose the pride in me that seeks to lead without You. I surrender my plans and my desires to You. Teach me to follow Your voice with clarity and obedience. Strengthen me to lead my family with humility, grounded in Your truth and guided by Your Spirit.

Reflective Verse

1 John 1:6 (ESV)
"If we say we have fellowship with him while we walk in darkness, we lie and do not practice the truth."

Day 2

Strong in Prayer, Strong in Purpose:
The Why and Where

Isaiah 55:11 (ESV)
"So shall my word be that goes out from my mouth; it shall not return to me empty, but it shall accomplish that which I purpose, and shall succeed in the thing for which I sent it."

I remember watching The Ten Commandments as a kid, maybe six or seven years old. Charlton Heston stood out, but it was a line from Yul Brynner that stuck with me: "So it is said, so it is written, so it shall be done." I repeated it constantly, convinced it was absolute truth. Later I realized I had it wrong, but in my mind it captured something deeper, when God speaks, it stands. That memory stayed with me, but I didn't always live like it was true.

As a man leading a family, I've had to wrestle with two questions over and over: Why am I doing this, and where am I going? Without those answers, I drift. I can be busy, active, even committed—but still off course. I've stepped into responsibilities before without clarity, assuming movement meant obedience. It doesn't. Without direction from God, it's just motion without purpose.

That tension exposed something in me. I was praying, but I wasn't listening. I would bring my plans, my ideas, my direction to God, but I wasn't waiting for His. Prayer became one-sided. And when you stop listening, you stop following. That realization hit hard. I wasn't lacking effort, I was lacking submission. I was leading, but not being led.

The shift came when I slowed down and made space to actually hear. Not rushed prayers, not distracted moments, but intentional stillness. God wasn't silent, I was just not listening. When I began to listen, direction followed. Obedience became clearer. Leadership became steadier. The why and the where were no longer mine to define, they were His to reveal.

God still asks the same question He asked in the garden: "Where are you?" He already knows, but He's calling for a response. I've had moments where I wanted to hide, to avoid, to stay silent. But a man cannot lead his family while running from God. The answer is not fear, it's repentance and obedience. If I'm going to lead, I must first listen, then follow, and then move forward with conviction in Christ.

Shepherding Value

Faithful Listening — A man leads his home by first listening to God and then obeying with clarity and conviction as a husband and father.

Reflect

1. Jesus calls you to listen and follow—where are you speaking more than listening in your relationship with Him?

2. Prayer without listening leads to self-direction—where is your heart resisting stillness before God?

3. Your family depends on your direction—how can listening to God reshape your leadership at home today?

Live It Today

Set aside five uninterrupted minutes today to pray and remain silent before God, then act on the first clear direction He gives you.

Personal Prayer

Lord, slow me down so I can hear You clearly. Strip away distraction and self-direction in my life. Teach me to listen with humility and to obey without hesitation. Lead me so I can lead my family with clarity, strength, and faithfulness in You.

Reflective Verse

Jeremiah 33:3 (ESV)
"Call to me and I will answer you, and will tell you great and hidden things that you have not known."

Day 3

The Sword of the Shepherd: Leading with God's Word

Psalm 28:7 (ESV)
"The Lord is my strength and my shield; in him my heart trusts, and I am helped; my heart exults, and with my song I give thanks to him."

I say it often, sometimes quickly, sometimes with intention: this is the day the Lord has made. There are days I whisper it in passing and others where I sit in it for a few minutes, letting it settle. But if I'm honest, there have been times when I've said the words without living them. I acknowledged the day, but I didn't fully step into it with God at the center. I moved forward in responsibility without first anchoring myself in Him.

That tension shows up quickly in leadership. As a husband and a father, I can step into the day relying on my own thinking, my own reactions, and my own strength. I can try to lead, guide, and protect without first being grounded in the Gospel. When I do that, everything becomes unstable. My patience shortens, my clarity fades, and my leadership becomes reactive instead of rooted. I begin to measure myself, my performance, and my outcomes instead of resting in redemption.

The turning point is always the same, I have to come back to abiding in Christ. Jesus made it clear that apart from Him, I can do nothing. That is not a suggestion; it is a reality. If I am not rooted in the Word of God, then I am not equipped to lead. The Word is not optional. It is the Sword. Without it, I am exposed. Without it, I am trying to shepherd without protection, without direction, and without truth anchoring my decisions.

When I take hold of the Word and actually live by it, everything shifts. I am no longer leading from my own strength but from His. The Sword is not something I carry occasionally, it is something I must carry daily. If I am going to stand for my family, protect my home, and lead with conviction, I must be anchored in Scripture and grounded in Christ. Anything less leaves me unprepared. A man cannot shepherd his family without the Sword, and a man cannot carry the Sword without first submitting himself fully to Jesus Christ.

Shepherding Value

Spiritual Readiness — A man leads his home by being daily equipped in God's Word, standing ready to guide, protect, and shepherd his family in truth.

Reflect

1. Jesus calls you to abide in Him through His Word—where are you neglecting daily engagement with Scripture?

2. Leading without the Word leads to self-reliance—where is your heart depending on your own strength instead of God's truth?

3. Your family looks to you for direction—how can you make God's Word more visible and central in your leadership at home?

Live It Today

Open your Bible today before leading anything else and apply one truth directly to how you guide your family.

Personal Prayer

Lord, anchor me in Your Word. Strengthen me to lead my family with truth, conviction, and dependence on You.

Reflective Verse

Hebrews 4:12 (ESV)
"For the word of God is living and active, sharper than any two-edged sword, piercing to the division of soul and of spirit, of joints and of marrow, and discerning the thoughts and intentions of the heart."

Day 4

The Heart of a Shepherd: A Man's Call To Serve

Ezekiel 36:26 (ESV)
"And I will give you a new heart, and a new spirit I will put within you. And I will remove the heart of stone from your flesh and give you a heart of flesh."

For a long time, I understood, at least on the surface, that I was worthy of God's love. I could quote Scripture, teach truth, and speak about grace with confidence. But deep down, something was missing. I didn't truly know it. Not in the way that changes you from the inside out. It stayed in my head but never fully reached my heart, and that gap affected how I lived and how I led.

That tension exposed itself in quiet ways. I could lead, serve, and do the right things, but still carry a subtle dependence on myself. I responded to God, but I hadn't fully surrendered to Him. I was operating with knowledge, but not transformation. I hadn't yet stepped into that deeper knowing, an intimate, lived understanding of His grace that reshapes everything.

The turning point came when that knowing became real. It was no longer something I could explain, it was something I experienced. That realization ignited something in me. It created a desire to know Him more, not out of duty, but out of response. My time in Scripture, my reflections, and even the work I do now are not routines, they are evidence of God actively shaping me. His grace was no longer an idea; it was a force changing my heart.

That shift forced a daily decision. I must empty myself so He can fill me. I must decrease so Christ can increase. This is not a one-time moment, it is a daily surrender. As I lead my family, serve in my roles, and step into responsibility, I do it not to earn His love, but because of it. A man cannot lead well without a heart transformed by grace, and a shepherd cannot serve without first surrendering fully to Jesus Christ.

Shepherding Value

Humility — A man leads his home with a heart shaped by God's grace, surrendering pride and serving his family with Christ-centered love.

Reflect

1. Jesus calls you to know Him deeply—where is your relationship with Him staying intellectual instead of transformational?

2. Grace reshapes the heart—where is your heart still holding on to pride or self-reliance?

3. Your family experiences your leadership daily—how can you lead them with greater humility and servant-heartedness today?

Live It Today

Identify one area of pride in your leadership today and intentionally surrender it to God through obedience in your home.

Personal Prayer

Lord, humble my heart and fill me with Your grace. Teach me to decrease so You may increase in my life and leadership.

Reflective Verse

Colossians 3:3 (ESV)
"For you have died, and your life is hidden with Christ in God."

Day 5

When Surrender Sparks Strength

Psalm 34:18 (ESV)
"The Lord is near to the brokenhearted and saves the crushed in spirit."

Humility is not something I stumbled into. It was forced out of me through pressure, through failure, and through moments where I could no longer pretend I had it all together. I lived like I was supposed to be strong on my own, like I had to carry everything without breaking. That mindset ran deep. The expectation to hold it together, to lead without weakness, to keep moving forward no matter what, it shaped how I saw myself and how I tried to lead.

Then everything broke. In 2008, life felt stable. I loved my family, I had joy, and I believed I had control. But 2009 came without warning, and my marriage ended. Divorce hit me hard. I was humiliated, ashamed, and overwhelmed with grief. The weight of it drove me into a dark place. One day, I pushed my car past 65 in a 50, staring at an oncoming truck, ready to end it. That moment exposed everything I was trying to hide, my failure, my pain, and my complete inability to carry my life on my own.

In that split second, God intervened. Not with force, but with a quiet redirection. My focus shifted away from myself, my shame, my collapse, and onto Him. That was the moment everything changed. It wasn't loud or dramatic, but it was real. I realized I was not the one holding things together. God was. That moment of surrender didn't fix everything instantly, but it marked the beginning of something deeper, dependence on Him instead of myself.

Since then, the refining hasn't stopped. The fire is real, and it exposes what doesn't belong. It is painful and slow, but it is necessary. What I've learned is this: Jesus is present in that fire. I am not alone in it. If I am going to lead my family, I cannot do it from a place of self-reliance. I must surrender daily, speak with Him, and depend fully on His strength. Real strength is not found in holding it all together, it is found in giving it all to Christ.

Shepherding Value

Dependence — A man leads his home by surrendering self-reliance and depending fully on God, allowing Christ to shape his leadership as a husband and father.

Reflect

1. Jesus calls you to surrender—where are you still holding onto control instead of turning fully to Him?

2. Internal struggle reveals dependence—what dominates your thoughts, your strength or your need for God?

3. Your family sees your response to pressure—how can you lead them by showing dependence on Christ instead of self?

Live It Today

Pause during a moment of pressure today and intentionally turn your thoughts and response toward Jesus instead of yourself.

Personal Prayer

Lord, I surrender my strength and depend fully on You. Lead me so I can lead my family in Your truth.

Reflective Verse

2 Corinthians 12:9 (ESV)
"But he said to me, 'My grace is sufficient for you, for my power is made perfect in weakness.'"

From MenOfTheShepherd.com
"When Surrender Sparks Strength" | February 4, 2025

Day 6

Sworn to Serve: The Oath of a Christian Man

2 Corinthians 12:9 (ESV)
"But he said to me, 'My grace is sufficient for you, for my power is made perfect in weakness.' Therefore I will boast all the more gladly of my weaknesses, so that the power of Christ may rest upon me."

There are moments where I have to stop and let this truth settle in. My sacrifices, the quiet ones no one sees, are not meaningless. They are not wasted effort. When I choose to serve my family with patience, when I hold my tongue instead of reacting, when I pray over my home in silence, something deeper is happening. But if I'm honest, there are times I want those moments to be noticed. There is a pull in me that wants recognition, something that affirms I'm doing it right.

That tension exposes a deeper struggle. I am called to serve, but part of me still wants to be seen for it. I can step into my role as a husband and father with the mindset of responsibility, yet still carry the desire for acknowledgment. That is where the battle is. The calling is clear, I am a guard, a protector, a man entrusted with leadership, but the strength to carry that calling does not come from me. When I try to lead from pride or self-reliance, I weaken the very role I've been given.

The turning point is understanding what I have actually been given. The sword I carry is not built on control or dominance. It is formed through faith, humility, and the Word of God. It is strengthened in the unseen moments, not the public ones. When I embrace that, everything shifts. Service is no longer about being recognized; it becomes about being faithful. The quiet acts of obedience become the place where strength is built and where trust in God takes root.

If I am going to lead my family well, I must accept the oath that comes with it. Not an oath spoken out loud, but one lived daily. I am called to serve, to stand firm, and to rely fully on God's strength. My role is not to be seen, but to be faithful. Real leadership is not proven in moments of recognition, but in the quiet, consistent surrender to Christ.

Shepherding Value

Humility in Leadership — A man leads his home by serving faithfully without seeking recognition, trusting God to strengthen him as a husband and father.

Reflect

1. Jesus calls you to serve in humility—where are you seeking recognition instead of serving Him faithfully?

2. The desire for acknowledgment reveals the heart—where is your heart relying on approval instead of God's strength?

3. Your family observes your consistency—how can you lead them through quiet, faithful service today?

Live It Today

Choose one act of service for your family today that no one sees and do it without seeking recognition.

Personal Prayer

Lord, teach me to serve in humility and depend fully on Your strength in my leadership.

Reflective Verse

Philippians 4:13 (ESV)
"I can do all things through him who strengthens me."

Day 7

Strong Hands, Humble Heart:
The Call of a Repentant Man

1 John 1:9 (ESV)
"If we confess our sins, he is faithful and just to forgive us our sins and to cleanse us from all unrighteousness."

Today's topic is a big one, and I need to start where the original starts: grab your sword. You are going to need it.

A man cannot lead his family with an unrepentant heart. If he tries, his hands will be weak, his will short and dull, and the fire within him will be nothing more than a smoldering spark. That is not enough to shepherd a home, protect a family, or stand firm before God.

The tension is simple and serious: repentance is not optional for leadership. It is the core, the foundation, the center of the burning desire God places in a man's heart. That fire is not emotional hype. It is the purifying fire on the altar of the soul, where God shapes, molds, and transforms a man. If I try to lead without repentance, I am trying to build a legacy on weakness instead of truth.

The turning point is understanding that repentance is not just feeling sorry. It is not a passing emotion after I mess up. Repentance is action. It is a willful, intentional movement toward God. It means recognizing sin, confessing it, apologizing where needed, asking forgiveness, committing to stop, and committing to change by God's help. This is not something to read and move past. This is something to live every day.

If you have not repented, the call is clear: start now. Seek God. Find a Bible-teaching church and do not walk this road alone. Repentance is personal, but it is not private in its effect. It shapes your family, your leadership, and your legacy. A repentant man leads with strong hands and a humble heart because he is not hiding from Christ—he is being transformed by Him.

Shepherding Value

Authenticity — A man leads his home with honesty and integrity, modeling repentance and alignment with God's truth as a husband and father.

Reflect

1. Jesus calls you to confess and turn—where are you trying to lead while avoiding repentance before Him?

2. Repentance is willful action—where is your heart settling for regret instead of real change?

3. Your family watches your response to sin—how can you model honest repentance in your leadership today?

Live It Today

Confess one specific sin to God today, ask forgiveness, and take one visible step to turn from it.

Personal Prayer

Lord, give me a repentant heart and the strength to turn from sin so I can lead my family in truth.

Reflective Verse

Acts 3:19 (ESV)
"Repent therefore, and turn back, that your sins may be blotted out."

Day 8

Pillar of Strength: Seeing The Face of God

Deuteronomy 31:6 (ESV)
"Be strong and courageous. Do not fear or be in dread of them, for it is the Lord your God who goes with you. He will not leave you or forsake you."

I've always been drawn to the story of Les Misérables. Growing up around NYC in the 80s and 90s, Broadway became something I kept returning to, and that story stayed with me. I saw it multiple times, and one line never left me: "To love another person is to see the face of God." That line always hit deeper each time, and I found myself wondering if it came from a place of real experience, something personal and powerful.

That idea carries weight when it comes to leading a family. As a husband and a father, you carry responsibility every day, and it is easy to let that responsibility become everything. You provide, protect, and lead, but in the middle of it all, your focus can shift. Your family becomes the center, and without realizing it, you begin to drift from Christ. That is the tension—you are called to shepherd your family, but you must never replace God with them.

The shift comes when you recognize that your leadership must flow from your relationship with Christ, not replace it. Your sword, the Word of God, is not just for protection, it aligns your heart. It keeps your focus where it belongs. When you lead with the Word, you are not just guarding your home, you are guiding your family toward Christ. Without that foundation, everything becomes unstable.

So when you look at your wife and your children, see more than responsibility. See God's grace, His calling, and His presence. Lead with courage, but stay anchored in Christ. Without faith, leadership collapses. With Christ as your foundation and His Word in your hand, you stand firm, serving your family with strength, humility, and purpose.

Shepherding Value

Faithfulness — A man leads his home with steady trust in God, grounding his leadership in Scripture and remaining anchored in Christ as a husband and father.

Reflect

1. Jesus must remain your focus—where are you allowing your responsibilities to replace your relationship with Him?

2. Leadership reveals your foundation—where is your heart drifting from Christ in the busyness of life?

3. Your family depends on your direction—how can you lead them with Christ as the true foundation of your home today?

Live It Today

Pause and refocus on Christ before leading your family today, then apply one truth from His Word in your actions.

Personal Prayer

Lord, keep my eyes fixed on You so I can lead my family with faith, strength, and truth.

Reflective Verse

Matthew 7:24 (ESV)
"Everyone then who hears these words of mine and does them will be like a wise man who built his house on the rock."

From MenOfTheShepherd.com
Pillar of Strength: Seeing The Face of God | February 7, 2025

Day 9

The Strength of an Intentional Shepherd:
Leading Through Christ's Power

2 Corinthians 12:9 (ESV)
"But he said to me, 'My grace is sufficient for you, for my power is made perfect in weakness.' Therefore I will boast all the more gladly of my weaknesses, so that the power of Christ may rest upon me."

Men, you have heard it before: you reap what you sow. As a shepherd of your home, that is not just a phrase, it is a responsibility. You are called to live your faith daily, not in theory but in action, leading your family with Christ's strength. But there is a tension here that cannot be ignored. You are told to be strong, to carry the weight, to lead with confidence, yet the reality is you are human, flawed, and living in a broken world. Your strength is not enough.

That truth confronts pride directly. You try to hold everything together, to be capable, dependable, and in control. The pressure builds, and eventually you face what you cannot handle. That moment exposes the truth, you are not sufficient on your own. The shift begins when you stop pretending and admit your need for God. That admission is not weakness; it is the beginning of real strength.

The world constantly pulls your focus toward self, what benefits you, what strengthens you, what elevates you. But you are not called to tune into that voice. You are called to take up the Word of God as your sword. Without it, you have no strength. When you rely on yourself, you fall short. When you rely on Christ, His strength carries you. This is where leadership changes, from self-reliance to dependence on Him.

When you surrender your weakness, Christ's power becomes visible. This is how you lead your family, not from pride, but from humility. God knows your struggles and still calls you to lead. He equips you, strengthens you, and produces fruit through you when you trust Him. Lead with His strength, sow faithfully in your home, and trust that the harvest will come through Christ.

Shepherding Value

Humility — A man leads his home by admitting his weakness and relying fully on Christ's strength as a husband and father.

Reflect

1. Jesus calls you to depend on Him—where are you still trying to lead in your own strength instead of trusting Him?

2. Weakness exposes the heart—where is your heart resisting surrender and holding onto self-reliance?

3. Your family follows your example—how can you model humility and dependence on Christ in your leadership today?

Live It Today

Identify one area of weakness today and intentionally rely on God's Word instead of your own understanding.

Personal Prayer

Lord, I surrender my weakness to You. Strengthen me so I can lead my family in Your power.

Reflective Verse

Philippians 4:13 (ESV)
"I can do all things through him who strengthens me."

Day 10

Radical Trust: Letting Go of Pride to Lead Like Jesus

Proverbs 3:5 (ESV)
"Trust in the Lord with all your heart, and do not lean on your own understanding."

Men, have you ever held something powerful in your hands, a tool, a weapon, a responsibility, and realized you didn't truly know how to handle it? Soldiers carry swords, but that doesn't mean they automatically understand them. It's the same with leadership in your home. Just because you are a husband, father, or grandfather doesn't mean you are leading well. You can stand strong in your role and still not know how to use what's been placed in your hands.

I've been there, standing confident, thinking I had it all together. But that strength only lasted as long as the applause. And when the applause faded, when life knocked me down, I realized there was no one to pick me up except Jesus. That moment exposes what you are really standing on. If your strength depends on recognition, it will not hold when pressure comes.

Relationships are messy. They are sticky, muddy, and complicated, and that is a good thing. The best ones are worth fighting for. But in the middle of that mess, there is one relationship that does not change, your relationship with Jesus. He is always present, even when you lose sight of Him. The problem is not His absence; it is your focus. Pride pulls your attention inward, filling your thoughts with what you want, what you deserve, and what benefits you.

That is where the shift happens. You must change what you are tuned into. Step away from that constant focus on yourself and pick up the Word of God as your sword. Cut through the muddy waters. It is hard, but it is necessary. Trust in the Lord with all your heart and stop leaning on your own understanding. Fix your eyes on Jesus, lay down your pride, and let Him lead. Real strength comes when you surrender, trust completely, and lead your family from a heart that follows Christ first.

Shepherding Value

Humility in Leadership — A man leads his home by surrendering pride and trusting God fully, allowing Christ to shape his leadership as a husband and father.

Reflect

1. Jesus calls you to trust Him fully—where are you still leaning on your own understanding instead of His?

2. Pride fills your focus—where is your heart centered on yourself instead of surrendering to God?

3. Your family follows your example—how can you lead them with trust in God rather than control today?

Live It Today

Identify one area where pride is driving your decisions and surrender it to God through obedience today.

Personal Prayer

Lord, remove my pride and teach me to trust You fully so I can lead my family in Your truth.

Reflective Verse

John 3:30 (ESV)
"He must increase, but I must decrease."

Day 11

Wielding the Weight: God's Power in Family Leadership

Philippians 4:13 (ESV)
"I can do all things through him who strengthens me."

Remember that scene in Avengers: Age of Ultron when the team gathered around, laughing and taking turns trying to lift Thor's hammer, Mjolnir? One by one, they strained, pulled, and joked, but none of them could move it. Then there was that moment when Captain America nudged it just enough to make Thor nervous. Still, no one could truly lift it. Only Thor could, and he did it effortlessly. Why? Because it was never just about strength. It was about being worthy to carry it.

That picture lands directly on your role as a man leading your home. God has placed a calling on you that can feel just as heavy, weighty, immovable, and at times impossible. Shepherding, providing, guiding, and serving your family is not light work. It presses on you. It exposes you. It reveals quickly whether you are trying to carry it in your own strength or relying on something greater.

I'll be honest, there have been mornings where that weight felt like too much. The pressure to provide, the challenge of patience, the decisions that affect everyone, it builds. It can feel overwhelming. But every time that weight pushed me to the edge, the same truth surfaced. When I brought it to God, when I laid down my pride and admitted my weakness, He met me there. Not with removal of responsibility, but with strength to carry it.

That is the shift. You are not called to carry your family in your own strength. You are called to lead through Jesus. What feels impossible becomes bearable when you surrender. What feels crushing becomes a privilege when you trust Him. Lead with humility, depend on His power, and remember, this weight was never meant to be carried alone. It is carried through Christ.

Shepherding Value

Humility enables strength — A man leads his home by admitting his need for God and relying on His power to guide, protect, and shepherd his family.

Reflect

1. Jesus calls you to rely on His strength—where are you trying to carry the weight of leadership on your own?

2. Pressure reveals your dependence—where is your heart resisting humility and holding onto pride?

3. Your family looks to your leadership—how can you model dependence on God in how you carry responsibility today?

Live It Today

Bring one burden you are carrying to God in prayer today and intentionally rely on His strength instead of your own.

Personal Prayer

Lord, I surrender the weight I carry and depend on Your strength to lead my family well.

Reflective Verse

Ephesians 2:8 (ESV)
"For by grace you have been saved through faith. And this is not your own doing; it is the gift of God."

Day 12

The Power of What You Consume:
Leading Your Family with a Clean Heart

Proverbs 4:23 (ESV)
"Keep your heart with all vigilance, for from it flow the springs of life."

When I was a teenager, computers were just starting to become a thing. Back then, they weren't sitting on desks, they filled entire rooms. One of the first lessons I learned about them was simple: "Garbage in, garbage out." If you put bad data into a computer, you'd get bad results out of it. No exceptions. The machine was only as good as the information it received. That truth stuck with me, and over time, I realized it wasn't just about machines, it was about my own heart.

What I allow into my life determines what comes out of me. It shapes how I lead, how I love, and how I show up for my family. I've had seasons where I let the wrong things in. Maybe not obvious sin, but junk, distractions, negative input, wasted time. And when I did, it showed. My patience wore thin, my focus slipped, and when my family needed strength, I was running on empty instead of being grounded in Christ.

The reality is, I cannot lead well if I'm not drawing from the right source. Jesus makes it clear that leadership doesn't come from my own strength. It comes from abiding in Him. When I try to operate on my own understanding, I fall into the same trap that has been there from the beginning, thinking I can handle things without God. That path never leads to life. It leads to distance, frustration, and failure in the very place I'm called to shepherd.

The world will always try to fill my mind with noise, but I am responsible for what I allow to stay. Every choice matters. What I watch, what I listen to, what I dwell on, it all shapes me. If I want to lead my family with clarity, strength, and truth, then I must guard what I consume and remain rooted in Christ. A clean heart does not happen by accident; it comes through intentional surrender and daily dependence on Him.

Shepherding Value

Discernment — What you allow into your heart shapes how you lead your family before God.

Reflect

1. Guarding your heart is essential—are you abiding in Christ daily, or allowing other sources to shape your thinking?

2. Letting in distractions affects your leadership—what are you currently allowing into your life that is weakening your focus or faith?

3. What you consume influences your home—how are you leading your family in filtering what enters your household?

Live It Today

Remove one source of distraction today and replace it with intentional time in God's Word.

Personal Prayer

Lord, purify what I take in and anchor my heart in You so I lead my family well.

Reflective Verse

John 15:5 (ESV)
"I am the vine; you are the branches. Whoever abides in me and I in him, he it is that bears much fruit, for apart from me you can do nothing."

From MenOfTheShepherd.com
The Power of What You Consume: Leading Your Family with a Clean Heart |
February 13, 2025

Day 13

No Good and Worthy Soldier…Training for Battle

Psalm 46:10 (ESV)
"Be still, and know that I am God. I will be exalted among the nations, I will be exalted in the earth!"

When my kids were younger, I noticed something that every father has experienced. I would start explaining something, and before I could even finish a sentence, they would cut me off. "I know, Dad." "You already told me." "I got it." At first, I pushed back. I reminded them that if they already knew, then there was no reason for me to continue. I would ask them, "If a glass is full, can you pour anything more into it?"

Over time, I stopped arguing. I let them sit in it. When they said they already knew, I moved on and said nothing. Eventually, something shifted and they began to listen again. Later, I told them that even when they think they already know something, they still need to be quiet and listen. There is always more to receive. That lesson was not just for them. It exposed something in me as well.

As men, we often approach God the same way. We rush in, ready to speak, ready to fix, ready to lead. But we have not learned how to be still. Jesus did not lead that way. He withdrew to quiet places. He stood silent when accused. He showed that strength is not found in constant action, but in surrender and attention to the Father.

No good and worthy soldier enters battle without training. Stillness before God is that training. It is where I acknowledge Him first, before anything else. Not my problems, not my plans, just Him. It is where I lay down control, step into the quiet, and prepare for the battles ahead. If I refuse that place, I will lead from noise instead of truth.

A disciplined man learns to be still before he moves. A shepherd who listens first will lead with clarity, strength, and conviction. If I want to lead my family well, I must enter the quiet, take my place before God, and prepare for battle the right way.

Shepherding Value

Stillness in Leadership — A shepherd leads best when he first learns to be still and listen before God.

Reflect

1. Being still before God shapes your leadership—are you intentionally setting aside time to listen to Him each day?

2. Rushing to speak can reveal a restless heart—where do you need to practice silence and surrender before God?

3. Leading your family requires preparation—how are you modeling quiet strength and dependence on God in your home?

Live It Today

Set aside uninterrupted time today to sit in silence before God before starting your responsibilities.

Personal Prayer

Lord, teach me to be still before You so I can lead with strength and clarity.

Reflective Verse

Luke 5:16 (ESV)
"But he would withdraw to desolate places and pray."

Day 14

Sharpened by the Storm:
A Father's Stand Against Darkness

Hebrews 4:12 (ESV)
"For the word of God is living and active, sharper than any two-edged sword, piercing to the division of soul and of spirit, of joints and of marrow, and discerning the thoughts and intentions of the heart."

Men, have you ever held onto something so tightly that it felt like it became part of you? A weight you could not let go of, even when it was too heavy to carry? That was me in the years after my divorce. I was newly saved, still learning how to walk with Christ, and suddenly my marriage was gone. I can still feel the weight of it, the distance from my children, the sharpness of the pain, and the reality that everything I thought I could hold together had fallen apart.

Even in that darkness, I did not let go of God. When my spirit was broken, I still prayed. When I felt weak, I still held onto His Word. When the enemy whispered lies, I still turned to Jesus. What I did not realize at the time was that I was not just surviving that season, I was being shaped by it. The Word of God became my sword, even when it felt heavy, even when I did not fully understand how to use it.

At first, it was unfamiliar. It felt like something I carried more than something I wielded. But I refused to let it go. Over time, that same sword changed in my hands. It became lighter, sharper, and part of who I am. Looking back now, I see clearly that it was not just something that helped me through, it saved my life. It became my weapon against darkness, my guide in leading my family, and my strength when everything else felt uncertain.

Now, as a husband, father, and leader in my home, I no longer fight for myself alone. I fight for my family. I stand for their peace, their faith, and their future. The strength I carry is not mine, it is His. And the sword I hold is not my own, it is the living Word of God, active and powerful in every battle I face.

Men, we are called to stand firm. To reflect Christ in our homes. To be men who are not defined by our own strength, but by the One who stands with us. Sharpen your sword. Stand your ground. And when darkness comes, let the light of Christ in you drive it back.

Shepherding Value

Surrendered Strength — A shepherd's strength is found in surrender to God, wielding His Word to lead and protect his family.

Reflect

1. Holding onto the Word shapes your walk—are you relying on Christ's strength or carrying the weight on your own?

2. Seasons of pain can sharpen your faith—how has God used hardship to shape your dependence on Him?

3. Leading your family requires spiritual defense—how are you using God's Word to protect and guide your home?

Live It Today

Spend focused time in Scripture today and apply one truth directly to how you lead your family.

Personal Prayer

Lord, strengthen me through Your Word and teach me to stand firm for my family in You.

Reflective Verse

Ephesians 6:17 (ESV)
"And take the helmet of salvation, and the sword of the Spirit, which is the word of God,"

Day 15

The Sword and the Walk:
Leading Through Failure and Grace

Hebrews 4:12 (ESV)
"For the word of God is living and active, sharper than any two-edged sword, piercing to the division of soul and of spirit, of joints and of marrow, and discerning the thoughts and intentions of the heart."

Men, one thing we all have in common is that we will fail. We will miss the mark, say the wrong thing, or make the wrong choice. I know I have failed more times than I can count, speaking too quickly, not listening well enough, or letting frustration take over when it should not have. Those moments leave a mark, especially when they affect the people we are called to lead and protect.

In those moments, the weight of failure can feel heavy. It can make you question whether you are fit to lead at all. The enemy uses that space to whisper that you are unworthy, that you have disqualified yourself, and that you should step back instead of stepping up. That pressure is real, and it can keep a man stuck if he allows it to take root.

But failure is not the final word. Scripture is clear that even the men God used greatly had moments where they fell short. Yet God did not abandon them, and He does not abandon you. He equips you with something that does not fail, His Word. The sword you carry is not limited by your weakness. It remains sharp, steady, and able to correct and guide you forward.

The danger is not failure itself, it is staying there. You cannot move forward while holding onto regret. The Word of God calls you to stand, to take hold of what He has given you, and to walk again. Not in your own strength, but in step with Him. Leadership is not proven in perfection; it is proven in perseverance.

You do not lead your family by knowing the Word alone, you lead by living it. Even when you feel unqualified, you move. You pray. You step forward. His strength meets you in that place. Pick up your sword, leave the past behind, and walk forward as the man God has called you to be.

Shepherding Value

Perseverance in Leadership — A shepherd does not stop leading after failure but continues forward in God's strength.

Reflect

1. Failure does not define your walk—are you trusting Christ to lead you forward instead of holding onto past mistakes?

2. Dwelling on regret can hold you back—where are you allowing failure to keep you from moving forward?

3. Your family needs consistent leadership—how can you take one step today to lead them despite feeling unqualified?

Live It Today

Take one intentional leadership action today—pray with your family or speak truth into your home.

Personal Prayer

Lord, help me release failure and walk forward in Your strength as I lead my family.

Reflective Verse

Galatians 5:25 (ESV)
"If we live by the Spirit, let us also keep in step with the Spirit."

From MenOfTheShepherd.com
The Sword and the Walk: Leading Through Failure and Grace | February 18, 2025

Day 16

Die Daily: Discipleship in the Mud

Luke 9:23 (ESV)
"If anyone would come after me, let him deny himself and take up his cross daily and follow me."

Want to win a Super Bowl? You practice. Want to win the World Series? You practice. Want to win a fight? You practice. Want to win your family? You practice. The greatest victories are not won in a moment, they are built through daily discipline. But there is a difference between being a warrior for yourself and being a warrior for Christ. Carrying the sword is an honor, but it begins with surrender.

That surrender is not theoretical, it is daily. John the Baptist said it plainly: "He must increase, but I must decrease" (John 3:30, ESV). That is the starting point for leadership in the home. Every morning requires a decision to lay down pride, selfish desires, and excuses. This is what it means to take up your cross. It is not a one-time commitment. It is a daily act of obedience that shapes how you live, lead, and love.

The problem is that the battle often begins within. The world pulls, distracts, and clings like mud. It slows you down and quietly takes ground if you stop moving forward. Discipleship is not occasional, it is constant. It is the unseen work of choosing obedience when no one is watching, removing what weighs you down, and preparing yourself before stepping into the responsibilities of the day.

Too many men want the outcome without the process. They want the armor without the sacrifice, the sword without the discipline, and the strength without the training. But leadership in the home is not built on intention, it is built on action. Daily action. Daily surrender. Daily obedience before God.

The war for your family is not won in big moments. It is won in the mud, in the daily grind of choosing Christ over self. Die to yourself. Pick up your cross. And lead your family from a life that is surrendered, disciplined, and grounded in Him.

Shepherding Value

Discipline in Leadership — A shepherd leads through daily obedience, building strength through consistent surrender to Christ.

Reflect

1. Taking up your cross daily requires surrender—are you choosing Christ first each day or holding onto control?

2. The battle begins within—what areas of your life are you avoiding daily obedience or discipline?

3. Your family follows your example—how are you modeling daily surrender and obedience in your home?

Live It Today

Choose one area today to deny yourself and intentionally obey God in that moment.

Personal Prayer

Lord, teach me to die to myself daily and lead my family through obedience to You.

Reflective Verse

Ephesians 6:11 (ESV)
"Put on the whole armor of God, that you may be able to stand against the schemes of the devil."

Day 17

The Intentional Shepherd: Leading with Pro-Active Love

Ephesians 5:25 (ESV)
"Husbands, love your wives, as Christ loved the church and gave Himself up for her,"

As men committed to Faith and Family First, the weight of leading a home can feel heavy. There are constant pressures, responsibilities pulling in different directions, expectations to lead well, and the quiet awareness that your family depends on your presence and direction. It is easy to drift into reacting instead of leading, responding only when something demands your attention instead of guiding with purpose.

This is where the concept of the Intentional Shepherd must be understood. It is not just an idea, but a calling that has been shaped over years of reflection, growth, and time in God's Word. Shepherding is rooted in Scripture, but this clarifies what it looks like for men today, to lead with purpose, strength, and conviction instead of passivity. An intentional shepherd does not wait for life to happen; he steps into his role and leads with foresight and direction.

At the center of this calling is pro-active love. This is not a reactive love that waits to be asked. It is a response to Christ Himself. Because He loved first, you choose to love first. That means stepping into the needs of your wife and children without hesitation, showing grace in the routine, strength in the challenges, and consistency in the unseen moments. This kind of love is not occasional, it is daily, deliberate, and sacrificial.

To lead this way, you must be equipped. The Word of God is not optional, it is your sword. It is what cuts through distraction, exposes truth, and protects your home from what seeks to divide it. Without it, you react. With it, you lead. This is not about force or control, but about discernment, protection, and direction rooted in Christ.

An intentional shepherd stands firm, grounded in the love of Christ and equipped with His Word. He leads with clarity, not confusion. If you are going to lead your family well, you must step into this calling, love first, and carry the responsibility God has placed in your hands with intention

Shepherding Value

Pro-Active Love — A shepherd leads by choosing to love first, reflecting Christ's love through deliberate action.

Reflect

1. Christ loved first—are you intentionally choosing to love your family before being prompted?

2. Intentional shepherding requires purpose—where are you drifting instead of leading with direction?

3. Your home needs active leadership—how are you stepping in to guide your family with love and clarity?

Live It Today

Take one unprompted action today to serve your wife or children in love.

Personal Prayer

Lord, teach me to lead as an intentional shepherd, loving first and guiding my family in You.

Reflective Verse

1 John 4:19 (ESV)
"We love because he first loved us."

Day 18

The Intentional Shepherd:
Leading with Purpose, Love, and Strength

Ephesians 6:17 (ESV)
"Take the sword of the Spirit, which is the word of God,"

The Intentional Shepherd is a man who has committed his life to following God's Word and leading his family with purpose, love, and strength. This is not passive leadership. It is rooted in a deep, personal relationship with Christ, where God comes first and everything else flows from that foundation. As a husband, father, and leader, he does not react to life, he steps into it with responsibility, guiding his family with clarity and conviction.

This calling is not optional. Every man is called to shepherd his home, to lead his wife and children with grace, humility, and unwavering love. Just as a shepherd carries a staff to guide and protect, the intentional shepherd carries the sword of the Spirit. The Word of God is not symbolic, it is active, shaping decisions, correcting direction, and guarding against spiritual danger within the home.

This path requires structure and focus. It is built on five essential expressions of leadership that define how a man lives this out daily: loving with **agape**, serving as a **friend**, building **relational** strength, pursuing **renewal**, and leading **transformation**. These are not abstract ideas. They are daily responsibilities that shape the culture of a home and the future of a family.

Over the next five days, this journey will move into each of these words, one at a time. Each day will focus on a single aspect of what it means to live as an intentional shepherd, bringing clarity to how you lead with purpose, love, and strength in your home. This is not theory. It is a daily application that builds a man who leads well.

The tension is that many men want to lead but lack direction. They want strength but avoid the discipline required to sustain it. Without intentionality, leadership becomes reactive, inconsistent, and weak. The intentional shepherd rejects that pattern. He chooses to lead with purpose, anchored in truth, and guided by the Word that equips him for every challenge he will face.

Shepherding Value

Intentional Leadership — A shepherd leads with purpose, anchored in God's Word and committed to guiding his family with clarity and strength.

Reflect

1. Leading begins with Christ first—are you rooted in your relationship with Him before leading your family?

2. Passive leadership creates instability—where are you reacting instead of leading with intention?

3. Your family depends on direction—how are you actively guiding them with purpose, love, and strength?

Live It Today

Identify one area in your home where you will lead intentionally and take action today.

Personal Prayer

Lord, anchor me in Your Word and strengthen me to lead my family with purpose and conviction.

Reflective Verse

Romans 12:2 (ESV)
"Do not be conformed to this world, but be transformed by the renewal of your mind, that by testing you may discern what is the will of God, what is good and acceptable and perfect."

From MenOfTheShepherd.com
The Intentional Shepherd: Leading with Purpose, Love, and Strength | February 21, 2025

Day 19

Man in Action – Agape: Loving as Christ First Loved Us

1 John 4:19 (ESV)
"We love because he first loved us."

Day 1 of Intentional Shepherd - Agape

Unconditional, sacrificial love that moves first. Want to win your family? You practice. Not in grand gestures alone, but in the quiet, unseen moments where love is tested and proven. I remember early in my marriage thinking love was flowers, date nights, and notes. Those matter, but they do not sustain a home. Real love is built when you are tired and still listening. When frustration rises and you choose patience, when you serve even when you feel empty.

Agape is not driven by feeling; it is a decision. It is choosing to love like Christ, sacrificially, unconditionally, without expecting anything in return. Jesus modeled this in every step. He washed the feet of men who would fail Him. He served without recognition. He gave Himself fully, not because we earned it, but because He chose to love first. That is the standard placed in your hands as a husband and father.

The tension shows up when leadership is tested. It is easy to love when things are smooth, but Agape shows itself when life is messy. Rehoboam ruled harshly and divided what he was meant to protect because love was absent from his leadership. Christ leads differently. He serves, sacrifices, and strengthens those under His care. That is the difference between reactive leadership and intentional shepherding.

I have learned that Agape means being first to forgive when I feel justified. It means showing up when no one notices. It means loving my family not based on how they respond, but because Christ has already filled me with His love. This love does not wait. It moves. It leads. It carries responsibility without needing recognition.

If you are going to lead your family well, this is where it begins. Not with control, not with authority, but with love that goes first. Agape is the foundation. Practice it daily, and you will build a home marked by strength, trust, and the presence of Christ.

Shepherding Value

Sacrificial Love — A shepherd leads by loving first, reflecting Christ through consistent, selfless action.

Reflect

1. Christ loved first—are you choosing to love your family sacrificially before being prompted?

2. Loving when it is difficult reveals your heart—where are you holding back instead of serving?

3. Your leadership shapes your home—how are you actively building trust and strength through Agape love?

Live It Today

Do one intentional act of service for your family without expecting recognition.

Personal Prayer

Lord, teach me to love first and lead my family with sacrificial, Christ-centered love.

Reflective Verse

Mark 10:45 (ESV)
"For even the Son of Man came not to be served but to serve, and to give his life as a ransom for many."

A Friend Like Jesus: Love That Stands the Test

John 15:13 (ESV)
"Greater love has no one than this, that someone lay down his life for his friends."

Day 2 of Intentional Shepherd — Friend

Love that sacrifices and remains when tested. Friendship is one of the greatest gifts a man can experience. A true friend walks with you through highs and lows, stands beside you in struggle, and celebrates with you in victory. But not every friendship is built to last. Some fade when pressure comes. Others break under the weight of betrayal.

I learned this over time through relationships I believed were strong. For years, I walked closely with two men, men I trusted, prayed with, and worked alongside. One was a minister working for me, the other a businessman I believed was grounded in faith. I brought them into my business, shared trust with them, and believed we were aligned not just professionally, but spiritually.

Then everything changed. A single phone call exposed what had been happening behind the scenes. These men had conspired to take my clients and undermine what I had built. In one moment, trust collapsed. The loss was real, but the deeper wound was betrayal. It forces a man to step back and ask a hard question: what is a true friend?

Jesus answers that question clearly. A true friend is not defined by convenience or benefit, but by sacrifice. "Greater love has no one than this, that someone lay down his life for his friends." This is not surface-level loyalty. It is a commitment that costs something. Jesus did not just speak this, He lived it. He knew betrayal was coming, yet He chose to love, serve, and ultimately lay down His life.

The tension is that men often measure friendship by what they receive. Christ flips that. A true friend is measured by how he loves, not what he gains. As an intentional shepherd, this is the standard you bring into your home. You do not withdraw when it gets hard. You do not love conditionally. You stand, serve, and remain steady for your wife and children.

If you are going to lead your family well, you must become this kind of friend. Not one shaped by past hurt, but one anchored in Christ. Jesus is the friend who never fails. Lead your family with that same loyalty, and you will build something that endures.

Shepherding Value

Loyalty — A shepherd leads with steadfast commitment, remaining faithful in love through every trial.

Reflect

1. Christ's friendship is sacrificial—are you choosing to love your family even when it costs you something?

2. Betrayal tests your heart—where are you allowing past hurt to affect how you love others?

3. Your family needs consistency—how are you demonstrating loyalty and presence in their lives daily?

Live It Today

Choose one way today to show consistent, sacrificial support to your wife or children.

Personal Prayer

Lord, make me a faithful and loyal man who loves and stands firm like You.

Reflective Verse

Proverbs 18:24 (ESV)
"A man of many companions may come to ruin, but there is a friend who sticks closer than a brother."

Day 21

Listening with Love: The Heart of Relational Fathering

Matthew 22:37–39 (ESV)
"You shall love the Lord your God with all your heart and with all your soul and with all your mind… You shall love your neighbor as yourself."

Day 3 of Intentional Shepherd — Relational

Love that listens, knows, and stays present. I have never been one to give gifts just to check a box. If I give something, I want it to mean something. I want it to last. That is how relationships are built, through real connection, intentional thought, and being fully present in the lives of those God has entrusted to me.

One day, my daughter Angelina and I were looking at Bibles together. As we flipped through the pages, she casually mentioned how much she loved taking notes, but the margins were too small. It was a small comment, easy to overlook, but I did not forget it. Months later, when she opened her gift, it was a Bible with wide margins. Her reaction was not about the gift itself, it was about what it represented. I had listened. I had seen her. I had remembered something that mattered to her.

That moment revealed something deeper. Shepherding is not about checking boxes or fulfilling obligations. It is about knowing your people. As men, it is easy to fall into providing, protecting, and moving on. But leadership that stops there is incomplete. Jesus did not lead that way. He knew His disciples. He understood their fears, their strengths, and their struggles. He invested in them personally.

The tension is that routine can replace relationships. You can meet needs without knowing hearts. You can provide without being present. But an intentional shepherd refuses that pattern. He listens. He pays attention. He engages. He leads from relationship, not distance.

If you are going to lead your family well, you must be present enough to know them. Your wife needs to be seen. Your children need to be heard. Real leadership is built on connection. When you listen, remember, and act, you build something that lasts far beyond the moment.

Shepherding Value

Intentional Presence — A shepherd leads by knowing his people, listening carefully, and engaging with purpose.

Reflect

1. Loving your family requires knowing them—are you truly listening and paying attention to their needs?

2. Routine can replace relationships—where are you going through motions instead of being fully present?

3. Your leadership shapes connection—how are you intentionally building deeper relationships in your home?

Live It Today

Ask one meaningful question today and listen without distraction to your wife or child.

Personal Prayer

Lord, help me to listen well and lead my family through intentional presence and care.

Reflective Verse

John 10:14 (ESV)
"I am the good shepherd. I know my own and my own know me,"

Day 22

Renewing the Mind: Sharpening Your Sword

Romans 12:2 (ESV)
"Do not be conformed to this world, but be transformed by the renewal of your mind, that by testing you may discern what is the will of God, what is good and acceptable and perfect."

Day 4 of Intentional Shepherd — Renewing

Transformation through daily surrender and alignment with God. There was a time when I believed I was ready to step into deeper leadership, even pastoral ministry. The desire was there, the intention was right, but something inside me resisted. I carried a quiet weight of unworthiness, measuring myself by my past instead of seeing myself through God's grace. That tension stayed with me longer than I wanted to admit.

Over time, I pursued opportunities, expecting doors to open, but they did not. The process exposed more than it affirmed. What felt like opportunity often felt like pressure, and I walked away from those moments thanking God for closing doors I thought I needed. Still, I prayed for renewal, not just in my thinking, but in my heart and direction.

Then came a moment I did not expect. I believed I had found clarity in pursuing missionary work, but something was unsettled. That became clear when my daughter spoke honestly and said she was feeling bitterness toward me. That moment cut deep. It exposed something I had missed, my desire to serve had moved ahead of my responsibility to shepherd my family. That realization forced a decision. I stepped back.

That decision was not loss, it was renewal. God used that moment to realign my thinking, my priorities, and my leadership. I saw clearly that I had been chasing what I thought was right instead of listening fully to Him. Renewal is not comfortable. It exposes, corrects, and redirects. But it brings clarity that cannot be gained any other way.

Renewing the mind is not a one-time event. It is a daily process of surrender, sharpening, and realignment. A man who refuses renewal will eventually lead from his own thinking instead of God's truth. But a man who submits to it will be shaped, refined, and prepared to lead well. Sharpen your mind with His Word. Let Him correct you. That is how you lead with clarity and purpose.

Shepherding Value

Renewal — A shepherd leads with clarity by allowing God to continually reshape his mind and direction.

Reflect

1. God renews your mind through truth—are you allowing Him to correct and redirect your thinking daily?

2. Resistance can block growth—where are you holding onto your own plans instead of submitting to God's direction?

3. Your family depends on aligned leadership—how are you modeling daily renewal and obedience in your home?

Live It Today

Spend intentional time in Scripture today and ask God to reveal one area that needs correction.

Personal Prayer

Lord, renew my mind and align my heart with Your will so I can lead my family rightly.

Reflective Verse

2 Corinthians 4:16 (ESV)
"So we do not lose heart. Though our outer self is wasting away, our inner self is being renewed day by day."

Day 23

Shepherding: The Legacy of Transforming Love

1 John 3:14 (ESV)
"We know that we have passed out of death into life, because we love the brothers."

Day 5 of Intentional Shepherd — Transformative

Love that changes lives and builds generational legacy. If you have been following these past few days, the pattern is clear, who you are, whose you are, and how you serve. As a man, husband, and father, you are called to protect and lead your family with the Word of God. That will look different for each man. Some lead through teaching, others through action, but all are responsible for shepherding their first church, the home.

That responsibility is not static. It is a house under constant construction. One moment you are grounded in truth, the next something breaks and demands your attention. Life does not pause for leadership. It tests it. That is where transformative love is revealed, not in controlled moments, but in the ongoing, imperfect reality of leading a home that requires steady care and attention.

The tension is that intentionality does not come naturally. Left unchecked, self-interest creeps in. I have seen that in myself more than I would like to admit. But when I choose to lead intentionally, I begin to see something bigger. The way I love, lead, and respond is not limited to today. It is shaping what comes next, my children, and the generations after them.

That is where the shift happens. Growth has not come from my own effort alone, but through what God has done in me, often through my family. Their presence, their words, and their needs have exposed areas that required change. That process is not easy, but it is necessary. It is how God transforms a man so he can lead with purpose instead of reaction.

Transformative love does not stop with you. When you submit to God, obey, and lead with intention, that impact moves forward. It becomes a legacy. Not built on perfection, but on consistent obedience and real change. If you are going to lead your family well, then lead in a way that outlives you.

Shepherding Value

Transformative Love — A shepherd leads in a way that changes lives and shapes future generations through Christ.

Reflect

1. Transformative love reflects Christ—are you allowing Him to shape how you lead and love your family?

2. Intentional leadership builds legacy—where are you choosing self-interest instead of generational impact?

3. Your influence extends beyond today—how are you leading your family in a way that will shape future generations?

Live It Today

Take one intentional step today that reflects long-term impact in your family, not just immediate results.

Personal Prayer

Lord, use my life to shape my family for generations through Your transforming love.

Reflective Verse

Colossians 3:10 (ESV)
"And have put on the new self, which is being renewed in knowledge after the image of its creator."

Day 24

The Intentional Shepherd's Heart:
Serving, Leading, and Loving Well

1 John 3:14 (ESV)
"We know that we have passed out of death into life, because we love the brothers. Whoever does not love abides in death."

I sat in my chair one evening, looking around at unfinished projects I had said I would take care of but had let slide. The kids were moving through the house, my wife was finishing up the dishes, and something did not sit right. It was not that I had rejected responsibility, it was that I had drifted into reacting instead of leading. I stepped in when things became urgent, but not before.

The idea of the Intentional Shepherd has been growing in my heart for years. It was not something formed overnight, but shaped through reflection, failure, and time in God's Word. Over the past several days, that growth has been unfolding more clearly, what it means to lead with purpose, love, and strength, and how easily that calling can slip into the background when I stop being intentional. That night exposed it. I was not neglecting my role, I was delaying it.

That moment forced a question. How often do I lead my family by reaction instead of intention? It is easy to believe I will step in when it matters, but the truth is that every moment matters. Shepherding is not about waiting for the storm, it is about preparing before it comes. It is about presence before pressure.

Jesus did not wait for the need to be obvious before He acted. He loved first. He served first. He stepped in before anything was asked of Him. That is the model. Not passive leadership, but proactive love that moves ahead of the moment. That means choosing patience before frustration, speaking encouragement before criticism, and stepping into the needs of my family before they have to ask.

The tension is that the world defines leadership through control and authority, but Christ defines it through service. He washed feet. He carried burdens. He led by giving, not demanding. That shift requires a decision. It requires small, daily steps, consistent action instead of waiting for the perfect moment.

Leadership in the home is not built on intention alone. It is built on action. If I am going to lead my family well, then I must move first, to love, to serve, and to lead before the moment demands it.

Shepherding Value

Pro-Active Love — A shepherd leads by taking initiative, loving and serving before being prompted.

Reflect

1. Christ loved first—are you stepping into leadership before your family has to ask?

2. Intentional shepherding requires awareness—where are you delaying action instead of leading with purpose?

3. Your family needs daily leadership—how are you consistently showing up to guide and serve them?

Live It Today

Take one intentional step today to serve your family before being asked.

Personal Prayer

Lord, help me lead with intention and love first, reflecting Your heart in my home.

Reflective Verse

John 13:14 (ESV)
"If I then, your Lord and Teacher, have washed your feet, you also ought to wash one another's feet."

Day 25

The Only Place I Want to Be

Psalm 73:28 (ESV)
"But for me it is good to be near God; I have made the Lord God my refuge, that I may tell of all your works."

I can still remember when my son was little and all he wanted was to be with me. No big plans, no toys, no distractions, just being near his dad was enough. Even now, as a grown man, he still makes time to be with me, and I value that deeply. But those early years stand out. You could see it in his face, joy, contentment, peace, simply because he was with me. Nothing else mattered.

One memory has stayed with me all these years. We were sitting in the back of our old minivan, the door open, waiting for a parade. Nothing special was happening. No music, no excitement. Just the two of us sitting there. But it was enough. He did not want to be anywhere else. And to me, that moment became one of the richest memories I have as a father, not because of what we were doing, but because of what it meant.

As I reflect on that, I realize that is exactly where I want to be with Jesus. No agenda. No performance. Just being with Him. The more I spend time in His Word and sit in His presence, the more I see it clearly, this is where my heart belongs. Not chasing outcomes, not trying to prove anything, but simply drawing near to Him.

That is where shepherding begins. It does not start with effort or performance. It flows from being close to Him. When I try to lead from my own strength, I drift. I start focusing on my own plans, my own reputation, my own thinking. I tune into what I want instead of what God desires. And when that happens, leadership becomes heavy, forced, and disconnected.

But when I stay near Him, everything changes. Love flows naturally. Direction becomes clear. Leadership is no longer about trying harder, it becomes an overflow of being with Him. If I am going to lead my family well, then I must stay close to my Shepherd. That is the only place I want to be.

Shepherding Value

Abiding Presence — A shepherd leads best when he draws near to God and leads from that overflow.

Reflect

1. Being near God shapes your leadership—are you leading from His presence or from your own effort?

2. Distraction pulls you away—where are you focusing on your own plans instead of drawing near to Him?

3. Your family sees what you pursue—how are you modeling a life that values being with God above all else?

Live It Today

Set aside quiet time today to sit with God without agenda or distraction.

Personal Prayer

Lord, draw me close to You so I can lead my family from Your presence.

Reflective Verse

John 15:4 (ESV)
"Abide in me, and I in you. As the branch cannot bear fruit by itself, unless it abides in the vine, neither can you, unless you abide in me."

Day 26

Everyday Shepherding: Teaching Without Words

Matthew 5:16 (ESV)
"Let your light shine before others, so that they may see your good works and give glory to your Father who is in heaven."

Back around 2012, I had a friend named Ken. He took his call to serve seriously, so seriously that he and his family moved into one of the poorest, most dangerous parts of the city. That became their place of ministry. My family and I supported them in prayer and service, and every time I drove through that neighborhood, I would slow down near his house and stop to pray. It was never anything public, just something between me and God.

One day, I drove right past without stopping. I did not think much of it until a voice came from the back seat: "Dad, we didn't stop to pray." That moment caught me off guard. I had never told them that was something I did. I never explained it or made it a lesson. They had simply seen it. When we stopped and prayed together, I realized something I had not fully considered, they had been watching all along.

That moment exposed a deeper truth. Shepherding is not limited to what you say. It is revealed in how you live. Your children see how you respond to stress, how you treat others, and whether you actually live out what you claim to believe. Many of those moments are not planned, but they still shape what your family understands about God and what it means to follow Him.

The tension is that it is easy to think leadership happens in big moments, devotions, teaching, or structured time. But most of it happens in ordinary life. In quiet decisions. In small acts of obedience. In moments when no one is watching, except they are. That is where faith becomes real to those around you.

If you are going to lead your family well, then your life must reflect what you believe. Not through performance, but through consistency. When your worship shows up in everyday life, your family will see it, and it will shape how they follow the Shepherd.

Shepherding Value

Everyday Worship — A shepherd leads through consistent, visible faith lived out in daily life.

Reflect

- Your life teaches your family—what are they learning about God from how you live each day?

- Small moments reveal real faith—where are you missing opportunities to show your trust in God?

- Your example shapes their walk—how are you intentionally living your faith where they can see it?

Live It Today

Pause in one everyday moment today to pray or act in faith where your family can see it.

Personal Prayer

Lord, help me live out my faith daily so my family sees You through my actions.

Reflective Verse

Psalm 46:10 (ESV)
"Be still, and know that I am God. I will be exalted among the nations, I will be exalted in the earth!"

Day 27

Strength in Intimacy: A Shepherd's First Prayer

James 4:8 (ESV)
"Draw near to God, and he will draw near to you."

Men, your family does not need perfect prayers, they need a shepherd willing to step into God's presence, even when the words do not come easy. Intimacy is not a word most men naturally embrace, but when you look at Jesus, the greatest Shepherd, what stands out is not just His power, it is His closeness with the Father. That is where real strength begins.

When I first became a Christian, I had no idea how to pray. It felt foreign, almost intimidating. I did not grow up in a home where prayer was normal. It was something I thought belonged to people who had it all figured out. But I wanted to learn, so I joined a men's prayer group early in the morning. The plan was simple, we would gather and pray. But I sat there in silence, day after day, unable to say a word.

One morning, I decided it had to change. I told myself I was going to pray out loud, no matter what. When the moment came, my heart was racing. One man prayed, then another, and then it was my turn. I froze. The silence hit, and I panicked. So I said the first thing that came to mind. I prayed about a fish I had read about the day before, a deep-sea fish that had been there all along, unseen. That was my first prayer.

It felt awkward at the time, but it taught me something I have never forgotten. Prayer is not about getting it right. It is about showing up. It is about speaking to your Shepherd, even when the words feel clumsy. Over time, that simple act turned into something deeper. Prayer became natural, consistent, and part of how I live. Not just in moments of need, but in everyday conversation with Him.

That is where intimacy forms. Not in perfection, but in presence. A man who walks closely with God will lead differently. His strength will not come from control or confidence in himself, but from being near his Shepherd. If you are going to lead your family well, it starts here, draw near, speak, listen, and stay close to Him.

Shepherding Value

Vulnerability — A shepherd grows stronger when he draws near to God with honesty and dependence.

Reflect

1. Drawing near to God requires humility—what is keeping you from praying openly and consistently?

2. Fear can silence your faith—where are you holding back instead of stepping into God's presence?

3. Your family learns from your example—how are you showing them what real prayer looks like?

Live It Today

Pray out loud today, even if it feels uncomfortable, and step into God's presence.

Personal Prayer

Lord, give me the courage to draw near to You and lead my family through a life of prayer.

Reflective Verse

Matthew 6:6 (ESV)
"But when you pray, go into your room and shut the door and pray to your Father who is in secret. And your Father who sees in secret will reward you."

Day 28

Faith and Family First
The Heart of a Man of The Shepherd

Psalm 46:1 (ESV)
"God is our refuge and strength, a very present help in trouble."

When the weight of life hits hard, shepherding your family starts with one step, steady, faithful, and fixed on God. There was a time when everything in my life broke apart. My marriage ended suddenly, right as I was beginning to understand what it meant to follow Jesus. What I thought was secure disappeared, and I could not see a way forward.

For years, I carried that weight. It was more than grief, it was the feeling that I had failed in the very place God had called me to lead. I turned to the church, expecting guidance, but what I found was limited. Some did not know how to respond. Others spoke without understanding. The help I needed never fully came from people.

But it came from God. In the quiet of my home, day after day, I prayed. Not long prayers, not complicated words, just a simple cry: protect my children and make me a strong father. That became the foundation. Not fixing everything, not restoring what was lost, but focusing on what remained, shepherding my children well.

Looking back now, I see what God was doing. Over time, my children grew strong in their faith. Not because I forced it, but because they saw it. They saw a man who kept going, who stayed on his knees, who trusted God when nothing else made sense. What I could not see then, God was building steadily.

This is the heart of shepherding. It is not built in visible moments or quick outcomes. It is built in steady, unseen faithfulness. It is choosing to keep moving forward, trusting God with what you cannot control. That kind of leadership shapes a home over time.

If you are going to lead your family well, then anchor yourself here. Faith first. Family first. Not in your strength, but in His. Step by step, prayer by prayer, trusting that what God is building will stand.

Shepherding Value

Perseverance — A shepherd leads through steady faith, trusting God's work even when results are unseen.

Reflect

1. When pressure comes, your foundation shows—are you relying on God or your own strength?

2. Faithfulness is often unseen—where are you being called to remain steady despite uncertainty?

3. Your family is shaped over time—how are you consistently leading them through prayer and trust in God?

Live It Today

Pray intentionally for your family today, trusting God with what you cannot control.

Personal Prayer

Lord, give me the strength to lead with steady faith and trust You in every step.

Reflective Verse

2 Corinthians 4:18 (ESV)
"As we look not to the things that are seen but to the things that are unseen. For the things that are seen are transient, but the things that are unseen are eternal."

Day 29

Forged in Fire
A Man's Journey in Shepherding His Home

Hebrews 4:12 (ESV)
"For the word of God is living and active, sharper than any two-edged sword, piercing to the division of soul and of spirit, of joints and of marrow, and discerning the thoughts and intentions of the heart."

Two years ago, I wrote down a few thoughts about what God was doing in my life. At the time, it felt simple, just capturing where I was and what I was learning. Looking back now, I can see those words carried more weight than I realized. They marked a process God was working through, not just in me, but in my family. What began as small steps of obedience has extended beyond what I expected, even reaching people I never thought would ask about Jesus.

That is when it becomes clear, this journey does not stop. God is always shaping, always refining. As men, we are not static. We are being formed. Like a sword that has been through battle, our lives carry marks. Some are deep, some are barely visible, but all of them tell the story of where we have been and what we have faced.

A sword that is used will be dull. It will take hits. It will wear down over time. But it is not thrown away, it is sharpened. The friction of the whetstone restores its edge. The polishing brings clarity. The same is true for us. The friction is time in the Word. The polishing is living out what God has done in you. The result is a life that reflects His truth, not just in what you say, but in how you live.

The danger is resisting that process. A man who avoids sharpening becomes dull. He loses clarity, direction, and the ability to lead well. But a man who steps into what God is doing, through trials, through pressure, through discipline, becomes stronger, steadier, and more prepared to shepherd his family.

Looking back, I see that what I thought were personal struggles were not just for me. They were shaping how I lead my family and influencing others who were watching. Your life is not separate from your leadership. It is the message. If you are going to lead well, then let God refine you. Let Him sharpen you. That is how you become the man He has called you to be.

Shepherding Value

Endurance — A shepherd grows stronger by allowing God to refine him through trials and sharpening.

Reflect

1. Trials shape your leadership—where is God refining you right now?

2. Resisting growth leads to weakness—where are you avoiding the sharpening process?

3. Your life is your message—how are your experiences shaping how you lead your family?

Live It Today

Spend time in Scripture today and apply one truth directly to your leadership.

Personal Prayer

Lord, refine me through every trial and sharpen me to lead my family well.

Reflective Verse

2 Timothy 4:2 (ESV)
"Preach the word; be ready in season and out of season; reprove, rebuke, and exhort, with complete patience and teaching."

Day 30

Leading Without Rushing: A Shepherd's Call to Wait

Habakkuk 2:3 (ESV)
"For still the vision awaits its appointed time; it hastens to the end, it will not lie. If it seems slow, wait for it; it will surely come; it will not delay."

Do you ever get ahead of yourself? You think you know what God is doing, so you move fast, only to realize you moved without Him. I have been there. It is not just frustrating, it is revealing. It shows how quickly urgency can replace obedience if you are not careful.

There was a time I was convinced I knew my calling. Missions in Thailand felt clear, urgent, and right. I researched, planned, and moved forward quickly. I was ready to sell my house and step into what I believed God had for me. But I was not actually following Him, I was following my own excitement. I rushed ahead, assuming clarity meant timing.

It took time to see the mistake. I lost money, lost time, and more importantly, I drifted from God in the process. I was moving so fast toward what I thought was His will that I stopped walking with Him. That was the real loss. It forced me to confront something deeper, trust is not proven in action alone, but in waiting.

This is where shepherding becomes real. You look ahead at your family and wonder what the future holds. Will your children follow God? Will your leadership produce something lasting? You want answers, direction, certainty. But your role is not to control outcomes, it is to lead faithfully where you are. God handles the timing.

Scripture shows this clearly. Abraham rushed and created unnecessary struggle. Paul waited and walked in obedience. The difference is not in the calling, but in the pace. A man who rushes creates confusion. A man who waits develops clarity.

If you are going to lead your family well, then you must learn to wait. Not passively, but faithfully. Walk with God at His pace. Lead with patience. Trust that what He has spoken will come in its time.

Shepherding Value

Patience — A shepherd leads with steady faith, trusting God's timing over his own urgency.

Reflect

1. Rushing reveals misplaced trust—where have you moved ahead of God instead of waiting on Him?

2. Waiting requires faith—how are you practicing patience in leading your family today?

3. Your pace sets the tone—how are you modeling trust in God's timing for those watching you?

Live It Today

Pause before making a decision today and seek God's direction instead of reacting quickly.

Personal Prayer

Lord, teach me to wait on You and lead my family with patience and trust in Your timing.

Reflective Verse

Proverbs 3:5–6 (ESV)
"Trust in the Lord with all your heart, and do not lean on your own understanding. In all your ways acknowledge him, and he will make straight your paths."

Day 31

The Surrendered Shepherd: The Power of Abandonment

Luke 14:26 (ESV)
"If anyone comes to me and does not hate his own father and mother and wife and children and brothers and sisters, yes, and even his own life, he cannot be my disciple."

What if the greatest strength you could offer your family was not found in control, but in surrender? For years, I said the Lord's Prayer without thinking. It was routine—something memorized and repeated. But after I truly surrendered my life to Jesus, those same words changed. They were no longer a script. They became real. They became a conversation with God that exposed something deeper—this prayer is a call to surrender.

Every line pushes you to let go. To trust God's provision, His forgiveness, His direction. That kind of surrender is not easy. As men, everything in us wants to hold things together. We want to lead, provide, protect, and control outcomes. But Jesus calls for something different. He calls you to release it. Not just your plans, but your need to control—even your family.

That tension is real. It sounds backwards. How do you lead by letting go? But that is the shift. When you hold tightly, you lead from fear. When you surrender, you lead from trust. You stop trying to force outcomes and start following God's direction. That is where real strength is found.

The Lord's Prayer exposes it clearly. Forgiveness requires letting go of pride. Trust requires releasing control. Obedience requires stepping back from your own will. You cannot shepherd well if you are gripping everything tightly. A shepherd listens to the Master and leads accordingly, not based on his own instincts, but on God's voice.

If you are going to lead your family well, it begins here. Surrender. Not once, but daily. Let go of control. Trust God fully. That is where your leadership becomes steady, clear, and rooted in something greater than yourself.

Shepherding Value

Surrender — A shepherd leads with strength by releasing control and trusting fully in God.

Reflect

1. Control can replace trust—where are you holding on instead of surrendering to God?

2. Surrender strengthens leadership—how does letting go change how you lead your family?

3. Your family follows your example—how are you modeling trust in God through your decisions?

Live It Today

Release one area of control today and intentionally trust God with it.

Personal Prayer

Lord, teach me to surrender fully and lead my family with trust in You.

Reflective Verse

John 3:30 (ESV)
"He must increase, but I must decrease."

Day 32

The Sword of Reckless Abandon

Romans 12:1 (ESV)
"I appeal to you therefore, brothers, by the mercies of God, to present your bodies as a living sacrifice, holy and acceptable to God, which is your spiritual worship."

There was a time in my life when I gave everything to something I thought would define me. In the 1990s, I built a 25,000-square-foot fitness facility in New York. Every dollar, every ounce of energy, every thought, I poured it into that place. I lived it. I breathed it. I was proud of what I had built and convinced I was where I was supposed to be.

But it consumed me. It demanded everything and gave nothing back. In the end, it left me empty, bankruptcy, broken relationships, and regret. What I thought would sustain me could not hold me. That experience exposed a hard truth. When you give yourself fully to the wrong things, you will be left with nothing that lasts.

That is where the shift begins. God does not call for partial commitment. He calls for full surrender. Not to something temporary, but to Him. He held nothing back, He gave His Son completely. That is the standard. Not a one-time decision, but a life lived in total surrender. When you abandon yourself to Him, you are no longer emptied, you are filled.

Scripture shows this pattern. Moses did not win by his own strength. When his arms grew weak, others stood beside him and held them up. Victory came through dependence, not independence. The same is true for you. Leading your family is not about building something in your own strength. It is about surrendering everything to God and trusting Him to work through you.

If you are going to lead your family well, you must decide where your life is anchored. What you give yourself to will shape what you become. Abandon yourself to God fully. Hold nothing back. That is where strength is found, and that is how you lead with clarity, purpose, and endurance.

Shepherding Value

Total Surrender — A shepherd leads with strength by fully giving his life to God and trusting Him completely.

Reflect

1. What you give yourself tdefines you—where have you poured your life that left you empty?

2. Surrender requires release—what are you still holding back from God?

3. Your leadership flows from your foundation—how are you anchoring your life fully in Him?

Live It Today

Surrender one area completely to God today and commit to trusting Him with it.

Personal Prayer

Lord, I give You everything. Lead me and use me to shepherd my family with Your strength.

Reflective Verse

John 3:16 (ESV)
"For God so loved the world, that he gave his only Son, that whoever believes in him should not perish but have eternal life."

Day 33

The Sword of Shepherding: Yielding to God's Call

Romans 6:16 (ESV)
"Do you not know that if you present yourselves to anyone as obedient slaves, you are slaves of the one whom you obey, either of sin, which leads to death, or of obedience, which leads to righteousness?"

It hit me the other day, one small decision can shape the way I lead my family. Not a big moment, not a major failure or success, but a simple choice. I saw it in how I spoke, how I responded under pressure, how I handled a moment that could have gone either way. Those choices are not isolated. They build something over time.

Look back at your last day. The words you spoke, the attitudes you carried, the habits you followed, those are not random. They are forming the man you are becoming. Leadership is not built in theory. It is built in repetition. What you allow today will define how you lead tomorrow.

The reality is simple. What you submit to, you become. If you give in to frustration, it grows. If you allow distraction, it takes ground. If you follow pride, it leads. But if you submit to God, if you choose obedience, He shapes you into something different. Stronger. Steadier. Focused.

I have caught myself saying I will change something later. But later does not lead. Today does. The habits you tolerate now will either strengthen your leadership or weaken it. There is no neutral ground. That is why obedience matters in the small moments. That is where change begins.

God is not distant from this process. He is present in it. When you feel weak, He is there. When you feel off track, He is there. But you have to choose to submit. Not once, but daily. That is not weakness. That is strength under control, directed by Him.

If you are going to lead your family well, then it starts with what you yield to. Choose obedience. Let God shape your habits, your words, and your actions. That is how you become the man your family needs.

Shepherding Value

Obedience — A shepherd leads well when he first submits daily to God's authority.

Reflect

1. Your habits reveal your direction—what are your daily choices forming in you?

2. Submission shapes leadership—where are you yielding to something other than God?

3. Your family watches your consistency—how are you modeling obedience in everyday moments?

Live It Today

Replace one negative habit today with a deliberate, Christ-centered action.

Personal Prayer

Lord, shape my habits and help me walk in daily obedience as I lead my family.

Reflective Verse

Acts 17:28 (ESV)
"In him we live and move and have our being, as even some of your own poets have said, 'For we are indeed his offspring.'"

Day 34

The Knight's Calling: Equipping With the Sword

Isaiah 41:10 (ESV)
"Fear not, for I am with you; be not dismayed, for I am your God; I will strengthen you, I will help you, I will uphold you with my righteous right hand."

I will never forget the moment my kids started singing in the middle of a grocery store. They were small, sitting in the cart, and without hesitation they began, "Jesus loves me, this I know, for the Bible tells me so." Loud. Unfiltered. And not concerned with who was watching. It caught me off guard, but it also revealed something deeper, what had been planted in them was already taking root.

That moment made something clear. Some battles are won long before they are ever fought. As fathers, we are not just raising children, we are preparing them. What we put into them now will shape how they stand later. Whether we are intentional or not, we are forming them for what is ahead.

The reality is that our children will face battles we cannot fight for them. We will not always be there to step in. That is why preparation matters. A soldier does not wait for war to begin before training. He prepares daily. Discipline, repetition, and consistency build readiness. The same applies in the home. Shepherding is not reactive, it is formative.

Jesus modeled this. As He walked toward Jerusalem, the disciples did not fully understand, but He did. He moved forward with clarity because His mission was set. That is leadership. Not avoiding the fight, but preparing for it. As a father, your role is not to remove every difficulty, but to equip your family to face it.

That is where the sword comes in. Not a physical weapon, but the Word of God. It is what strengthens, guides, and grounds your children when you are not there. Through prayer, example, discipline, and truth, you are shaping them. One day, they will stand on their own. What you have placed in their hands will determine how they stand.

If you are going to lead your family well, then focus on preparation. Be intentional. Invest daily. What you build now will carry forward long after you step back.

Shepherding Value

Preparation — A shepherd equips his family with truth and discipline to stand strong in future battles.

Reflect

1. Preparation shapes outcomes—what are you actively building into your children today?

2. Leadership requires intention—where are you relying on chance instead of consistent training?

3. Your influence extends forward—how are you equipping your family with God's Word to stand on their own?

Live It Today

Spend time today teaching or modeling one truth from Scripture to your family.

Personal Prayer

Lord, give me wisdom to prepare my family well and strength to lead them with Your truth.

Reflective Verse

Ephesians 6:17 (ESV)
"And take the helmet of salvation, and the sword of the Spirit, which is the word of God,"

Day 35

Leading with a Sharpened Sword

1 John 1:7 (ESV)
"But if we walk in the light, as he is in the light, we have fellowship with one another, and the blood of Jesus his Son cleanses us from all sin."

Your family does not need a shepherd tomorrow, they need one today. The battle is not coming, it is already here. The question is whether you are prepared or not. I remember hearing that Arnold Schwarzenegger trained no matter what, even when he was sick, because it was ingrained in him. That level of discipline stood out, not because of fitness, but because it reflects something deeper. Training determines readiness.

That same principle applies spiritually. You do not become strong when the pressure hits. You become strong through daily preparation before it does. Real soldiers train constantly because when the fight comes, there is no time to figure things out. You either know what to do, or you do not. As a man leading his home, that reality applies directly to you.

I have seen this play out in my own home. My children are not just exposed to faith, they live it. Prayer, Scripture, and conversation about God are part of everyday life. That did not happen by accident. It came through consistency. Through repetition. Through daily sharpening. What is built over time becomes natural.

When that discipline is missing, something else takes over. Weakness shows up. Distraction increases. Sin becomes familiar, and eventually unnoticed. You begin to drift without realizing it. That is the real danger, not obvious failure, but slow, unnoticed decline. Without sharpening, you lose clarity. Without clarity, you lose direction.

The solution is not complicated, but it is demanding. Stay in the Word. Pray consistently. Surround yourself with men who are doing the same. Accountability strengthens you. Isolation weakens you. A man does not sharpen himself alone. He needs others who will challenge him and keep him focused.

If you are going to lead your family well, then train daily. Do not rely on intention, build discipline. Stay sharp. Stay ready. That is how you step into the fight prepared.

Shepherding Value

Sharpen — A shepherd maintains strength through daily discipline in God's Word, prayer, and accountability.

Reflect

1. Readiness comes from discipline—where have you stopped training spiritually?

2. Drift happens slowly—what areas of your life show signs of neglect or weakness?

3. Strength is reinforced in community—who is sharpening you and holding you accountable?

Live It Today

Spend focused time in Scripture and connect with one man who strengthens your faith.

Personal Prayer

Lord, sharpen me daily and give me discipline to lead my family with strength and clarity.

Reflective Verse

Proverbs 27:17 (ESV)
"Iron sharpens iron, and one man sharpens another."

Day 36

The One Big Thing: Keeping God at the Center of Your Leadership

2 Corinthians 5:9 (ESV)
"So whether we are at home or away, we make it our aim to please him."

You can work hard, provide, and check every box, but if everything is centered in the wrong place, it will not last. As a husband and father, your daily checklist matters. The small things, your words, your tone, your responses, shape your home more than you realize. Saying "I love you," owning your mistakes, asking for forgiveness, these are not minor actions. They are leadership in motion.

But the real issue is not the list itself. It is what sits at the top of it. What drives everything else. That is the difference between movement and direction. You can be busy, productive, and still be off course. The question is simple, what is your One Big Thing?

For Paul, it was clear. His aim was to please God. Not occasionally, not when convenient, but consistently. That focus gave everything else alignment. When that priority is right, your leadership becomes clear. When it is off, you drift, even if you are doing good things.

I have seen that drift personally. There was a time I was so focused on doing things for God that I lost focus on being with Him. The activity looked right, but the foundation was off. I was moving fast, making plans, ready to act, but I was not centered. That shift matters more than anything else. God is not looking for output first. He is looking for alignment.

That is where the Holy Spirit comes in. You are not meant to lead on your own. You are meant to be guided. Through prayer, through the Word, through listening. When you stay connected, your decisions change. Your leadership changes. Your home changes.

If you are going to lead your family well, then define your One Big Thing clearly. Keep God at the center. Make it your aim to please Him. Everything else flows from that.

Shepherding Value

Master Ambition — A shepherd leads with clarity when his primary aim is to please God above all else.

Reflect

1. Your priorities define your direction—what is truly at the top of your daily focus?

2. Activity can mask drift—where are you doing good things but losing focus on God?

3. Alignment strengthens leadership—how are you seeking God's direction in your decisions?

Live It Today

Set your focus intentionally on pleasing God in one key decision today.

Personal Prayer

Lord, keep my focus on You and guide my leadership so I live to please You.

Reflective Verse

Luke 11:13 (ESV)
"If you then, who are evil, know how to give good gifts to your children, how much more will the heavenly Father give the Holy Spirit to those who ask him!"

Day 37

Forgiveness: The Hard Road to Freedom

Ephesians 4:32 (ESV)
"Be kind to one another, tenderhearted, forgiving one another, as God in Christ forgave you."

Unforgiveness is not neutral. It carries weight, and that weight does not stay contained, it spreads. You can ignore it, justify it, or carry it like it gives you strength, but it works against you. It shapes your thinking, your responses, and ultimately your leadership. If you are leading a family, that weight does not stop with you, it reaches them as well.

I have lived through that reality. There were two moments in my life that cut deep. One involved a business situation where trust was broken and the outcome cost me financially. The other was personal, affecting my family in a way that left lasting damage. In both cases, forgiveness was not immediate. I held onto the offense. I carried it, and over time, it became part of how I responded to life.

But that is the trap. Unforgiveness does not strengthen you, it weakens you. It narrows your perspective and hardens your heart. It keeps you tied to what happened instead of allowing you to move forward. At some point, it became clear that holding onto it was not aligned with walking with God. The issue was no longer about what others had done. It was about my response.

Forgiveness does not mean excusing what happened. It does not mean restoring trust where it has been broken. It means releasing control over the outcome and trusting God with justice. That is where the shift happens. It moves from being about them to being about your relationship with God.

This is not a one-time decision. It is a process. Some days it feels complete, other days it resurfaces. But each step toward forgiveness removes weight. Each decision to release it strengthens your ability to lead with clarity and steadiness.

If you are going to lead your family well, then you cannot carry what will undermine you. Let it go. Not because it is easy, but because it is necessary. That is where freedom begins.

Shepherding Value

Forgiveness — A shepherd leads with strength by releasing bitterness and trusting God with justice.

Reflect

1. Unforgiveness shapes your leadership—what are you still holding onto?

2. Bitterness affects others—how is your response influencing your family?

3. Freedom requires release—what step can you take to begin letting go today?

Live It Today

Identify one offense and intentionally release it to God in prayer.

Personal Prayer

Lord, help me release bitterness and lead my family with a heart shaped by Your grace.

Reflective Verse

Matthew 6:12 (ESV)
"And forgive us our debts, as we also have forgiven our debtors."

From MenOfTheShepherd.com
Forgiveness: The Hard Road to Freedom | March 20, 2025

Day 38

Faith in the Fire: Learning to Lead Without the Fight

Exodus 14:14 (ESV)
"The Lord will fight for you, and you have only to be silent."

The instinct to fight runs deep. When something feels off, disrespect, pressure, conflict, the natural response is to push back and prove yourself. But not every battle is yours to fight. Some are distractions, and stepping into them only pulls you off course.

I have been there. A situation at work turned into something it did not need to be. I had experience, a solid track record, and no real issues, but I felt pushed and micromanaged. Instead of stepping back, I stepped in. I wrote a careful, professional response, thinking it would bring clarity and resolution. It did not. The situation escalated, and the outcome fell short of what I expected.

Looking back, the issue was not the other person. It was my response. I made it about proving a point instead of trusting God. I reacted out of frustration instead of stepping back in faith. What felt justified did not produce anything of value. It only revealed how quickly pride can take over when left unchecked.

Scripture shows a different path. When Israel was denied passage, they had every reason to push forward. Instead, they turned away. Not because they were weak, but because they trusted God's direction over their own impulse. That is leadership, knowing when not to engage.

The challenge is recognizing the difference between necessary battles and unnecessary ones. Many conflicts come from a desire to be right, to be heard, or to defend position. But those motivations often lead away from where God is directing you. Following Him requires restraint. It requires trust.

If you are going to lead your family well, then you must learn when to step back. Not every situation requires a response. Sometimes the stronger move is silence. Sometimes the wiser path is walking away. That is not weakness, it is alignment with God's lead.

Shepherding Value

Obedience — A shepherd leads with strength by following God's direction instead of reacting out of pride.

Reflect

1. Not every battle is yours—where are you engaging in conflict you should release?

2. Reaction reveals priorities—are your responses driven by pride or trust in God?

3. Leadership requires restraint—how can you model calm, controlled responses in your home?

Live It Today

Step back from one unnecessary conflict and choose prayer over reaction.

Personal Prayer

Lord, help me trust Your direction and lead with wisdom instead of reacting in pride.

Reflective Verse

James 1:19–20 (ESV)
"Know this, my beloved brothers: let every person be quick to hear, slow to speak, slow to anger; for the anger of man does not produce the righteousness of God."

Day 39

Stop Shepherding by Doing—Start Being with God

Psalm 37:4 (ESV)
"Delight yourself in the Lord, and he will give you the desires of your heart."

You can stay busy, stay productive, and still be off track. That is the danger. There was a season when I was convinced I was moving in the right direction. I was preparing for missions, ready to sell my house, make major changes, and step fully into what I believed was God's plan. Everything looked aligned from the outside.

But underneath it, something was missing. I was moving fast, making plans, and pushing forward, but I was not grounded in my relationship with God. I was focused on doing for Him, not being with Him. At some point, it became clear that the activity was replacing the relationship. What looked like obedience was actually misalignment.

That is where many men get it wrong. Action feels right. Responsibility feels productive. But movement is not the same as direction. You can build momentum and still be heading away from what matters most. God is not asking for output first, He is calling for relationship.

Scripture makes that clear. God walked with Abraham. The calling was not separate from the relationship, it came from it. Without that connection, decisions become driven by assumption instead of direction. That is when you start leading from your own understanding instead of God's.

The correction is simple, but it requires discipline. Stop measuring your leadership by what you do. Start measuring it by how closely you are walking with Him. When that is right, everything else aligns. When it is not, everything else eventually breaks down.

If you are going to lead your family well, then start here. Be with God first. Not for answers, not for outcomes, but for Him. That is the foundation your leadership depends on.

Shepherding Value

Intimacy — A shepherd leads effectively only when his relationship with God comes first.

Reflect

1. Activity can replace connection—are you doing for God more than being with Him?

2. Direction flows from relationship—how consistent is your time with God?

3. Leadership depends on foundation—are you leading from intimacy or routine?

Live It Today

Set aside uninterrupted time to be with God without focusing on tasks or outcomes.

Personal Prayer

Lord, draw me closer to You so I lead my family from a real relationship with You.

Reflective Verse

Matthew 6:33 (ESV)
"But seek first the kingdom of God and his righteousness, and all these things will be added to you."

Day 40

Living the Life Your Family Needs Today: Live the Amen

Galatians 2:20 (ESV)
"I have been crucified with Christ. It is no longer I who live, but Christ who lives in me. And the life I now live in the flesh I live by faith in the Son of God, who loved me and gave himself for me."

There comes a point where faith cannot stay private. It moves beyond belief and becomes visible. Not in words, but in how you live. Your family does not need a version of you that tries harder, they need a man who lives surrendered. That is the shift. From effort to surrender. From saying to living.

I have had to face that myself. This is not theory. It is ongoing. There have been moments where I realized I was trying to lead from my own strength, trying to manage outcomes, trying to fix what I could not control. And in those moments, the pressure builds. The gap becomes clear, what is needed and what I can actually produce do not match.

That is where the truth of Galatians 2:20 becomes real. Leadership does not come from your strength. It comes from Christ living through you. When you try to carry it alone, you run out. When you surrender, something changes. You stop leading from your own will and begin responding to His.

This is not a one-time decision. It is daily. It starts in the morning, choosing to give the day over to God before anything else takes hold. And it ends at night, recognizing whether you walked in that surrender or not. That is the "Amen." Not a word, but a life that reflects what you committed to.

Your family sees this. They recognize whether your faith is active or passive. Whether your words align with your actions. Whether your leadership is rooted in something real or just routine. If Christ is not leading through you, something else is. That is the reality.

If you are going to lead your family well, then stop relying on your own reserves. Surrender early. Stay aligned. Let Christ live through you. That is where strength comes from, and that is what your family needs.

Shepherding Value

Intentional Surrender — A shepherd leads effectively when he lives daily through Christ, not his own strength.

Reflect

1. Leadership reveals source—are you leading from your own strength or Christ in you?

2. Daily surrender builds consistency—how are you intentionally giving your day to God?

3. Your family observes alignment—do your actions reflect what you claim to believe?

Live It Today

Start your day by intentionally surrendering your will to God before anything else.

Personal Prayer

Lord, live through me today so I lead my family from Your strength, not my own.

Reflective Verse

Romans 12:1 (ESV)
"I appeal to you therefore, brothers, by the mercies of God, to present your bodies as a living sacrifice, holy and acceptable to God, which is your spiritual worship."

Day 41

Strategic Surrender: It's Where Warriors Are Forged

Psalm 62:5 (ESV)
"For God alone, O my soul, wait in silence, for my hope is from him."

The other night, my 21-year-old son built a fire. No reason. No plan. He just wanted to sit outside like we used to. He grabbed some s'mores, and we sat there together. In the middle of the laughter, everything slowed down. Then came a moment where no one spoke. Just the sound of the fire cracking and the warmth pushing back the night. That silence did something. It woke something up.

Men, when was the last time you sat still long enough to hear from God? Most of us don't. Life is loud. Work, responsibilities, stress, constant movement, it never stops. And somewhere in all that noise, the voice we need the most gets drowned out. The problem is not just that we are busy. It is that we are leading while disconnected. And you cannot lead your family well if you are not hearing from the One who leads you.

I have seen this in my own life. When things get busy, I push forward. I get things done. But something starts to fade. The desire to be with God weakens, and I begin leading from my own strength. That always ends the same way, I hit a wall. That is when I have to step back and remember: it is not about me. It is Christ in me.

Scripture shows this pattern clearly. Noah built in quiet obedience for years before anything happened. Abraham waited in silence before the promise came. Moses spent decades in the wilderness before God spoke. Even between the Old and New Testaments, there were years of silence before Jesus came. God does His deepest work in the stillness.

We resist silence because it feels unproductive. But silence is where surrender happens. It is where our hearts are shaped, where pride is quieted, and where we begin to hear again. "Be still, and know that I am God." That is not a weakness. That is alignment.

Strategic surrender means choosing stillness on purpose. It means stepping out of the noise so God can lead. It means trusting that what He is doing in the quiet matters more than what we are doing in the noise.

If you want to lead with strength, you must first learn to be still. That is where the fire is kept alive. That is where your leadership is forged.

Shepherding Value

Stillness — A shepherd leads with clarity and strength when his heart is quiet before God.

Reflect

1. Noise blocks direction—what is currently drowning out your ability to hear God?

2. Silence reveals dependence—when do you intentionally create space to listen?

3. Leadership flows from alignment—how does stillness strengthen your role in your home?

Live It Today

Set aside 10–15 minutes of uninterrupted silence and sit before God without distraction.

Personal Prayer

Father, quiet my heart so I can hear You clearly and lead from Your strength.

Reflective Verse

Psalm 46:10 (ESV)
"Be still, and know that I am God."

Day 42

Naked in the Light: Leading from Silence and Strength

Galatians 5:16 (ESV)
"But I say, walk by the Spirit, and you will not gratify the desires of the flesh."

I remember the day I stopped trying to be liked. It wasn't pride, it was clarity. I was tired of performing, tired of trying to be "good enough" for people who didn't matter, and tired of carrying the weight of expectations that kept shifting. There was a quiet resentment building in me, and I didn't even see it until the Spirit brought it into the light. Not some abstract idea, but full exposure, like standing with nothing left to hide, and somehow, I wasn't ashamed. I was free.

I think about when my kids were little, running around with no fear, no shame, just joy. But somewhere along the way, that changes. The world teaches them to cover up, to perform, to protect themselves. And we do the same. We stack layers, "I've got this," "I'm fine," "don't show weakness", while the Spirit is working to strip it all off. Not to embarrass us, but to free us from what's been suffocating us for years.

Men, we can't lead our families if we're still chasing approval from people. That need, whether from a boss, a friend, a father, or anyone else, chokes our identity in Christ. It keeps us stuck in pride, insecurity, and fear. But when we step into the light of Jesus, all that junk, control, anger, defensiveness, the need to be right, starts to lose its power. You don't have to prove yourself anymore. That's where leadership begins.

Silence is where that shift happens. Not empty silence, but the kind that forces you to stop talking, stop pretending, and listen. "Be still, and know that I am God." In that stillness, everything changes. You remember that God is God, and you are not. That's not weakness. That's strength. That's where the Spirit exposes what's real and strips away what doesn't belong.

I lived for years believing I was unworthy to serve. I thought I was being humble, but I was really hiding, afraid of being seen and judged. When the Spirit exposed that lie, everything shifted. I wasn't unworthy to serve God, I was just afraid of not being enough for people. When He spoke, I stood in His light, exposed but confident, not in myself but in Him. That's when I stopped hiding. That's when I began to lead.

Shepherding Value

God-given worth — True confidence comes when a man stops seeking the approval of others and begins walking in the identity and worth God has already given him in Christ.

Reflect

1. The Spirit calls you to walk in truth, not approval—are you following Him or still seeking acceptance from people?

2. God brings everything into the light—what are you still hiding instead of bringing fully before Him?

3. Your identity is rooted in Christ, not people—how is your fear of not being enough shaping how you lead your family today?

Live It Today

Sit in complete silence before God for five minutes and listen without distraction.

Personal Prayer

Lord, strip away every layer I'm hiding behind and let me stand in Your light with confidence in You.

Reflective Verse

Psalm 46:10 (ESV)
"Be still, and know that I am God."

Day 43

Stop Playing God—Start Leading Like a Shepherd

John 3:30 (ESV)
"He must increase, but I must decrease."

In 2008, I was called. God shook me awake in a way that made it clear I couldn't keep living the same. The very next year, in 2009, my wife left. It blindsided me. I wasn't just grieving a marriage, I was grieving a future I thought was already set. For years, I walked through the wreckage, trying to make sense of it, trying to hold something together that was already gone. But through it all, God never left. He stayed.

That season became the fire where God began to forge something deeper in me. He brought the sword, cutting through the noise so I could finally see Him clearly. Sometimes that sword came through heartache. Sometimes it came through silence. But it forced a decision. It divided what I thought I controlled from what only He could carry. And in that place, I chose to lean in instead of pulling away.

I stepped into ministry. I went to school, became ordained, and served in churches, healthcare, hospice, and the community. But the real work wasn't in the titles, it was in what God stripped away. Looking back, I can see how often I leaned on people instead of the Lord. Others tried to fix things, to step in, to help, and I let them. And worse, I've done the same to others, stepping into their situations when I should have stepped back and let God do His work.

When we move without the Spirit, we get in the way. When we think we know better than God's process, we slow down what He's trying to build. And if we're honest, that's us trying to take His place. That's us increasing while He decreases. But John 3:30 isn't a suggestion, it's the line that defines everything. If we're going to lead like Jesus, we have to follow Him first.

Real leadership begins with submission. Not stepping ahead, not trying to fix everything, but walking behind Christ and pointing others to Him. I had to learn the hard way that I wasn't called to be the savior of my family, I was called to lead them to the Savior. When I finally got out of the way and let God lead, everything changed. That's where strength begins. That's where a shepherd is formed.

Shepherding Value

Submission — Strong shepherd leadership begins when a man steps back, submits to God's authority, and follows Christ instead of trying to control outcomes.

Reflect

1. Jesus must increase as you decrease—are you following His lead or still trying to control what only He can lead?

2. God works through His process, not your pressure—where are you relying on others instead of trusting Him?

3. You are called to point your family to the Savior—how is trying to fix what isn't yours affecting how you lead them right now?

Live It Today

Identify one situation you've been trying to control and surrender it to God in prayer today.

Personal Prayer

Lord, help me step back and follow You fully. Teach me to lead by trusting Your authority, not my own.

Reflective Verse

Mark 10:34 (ESV)
"And they will mock him and spit on him, and flog him and kill him. And after three days he will rise."

Day 44

First Connection, Then Direction

John 14:15 (ESV)
"If you love me, you will keep my commandments."

When I first started as a Christian, prayer was hard. Real hard. I grew up in a Roman Catholic home where the only people I heard pray were priests. We had memorized prayers, but no one ever showed me how to speak to God from the heart. Then I stepped into a Protestant church and found myself in a men's prayer group at 6 a.m. every Wednesday. Three to six guys, praying around the circle, led by the Spirit. And me? I sat there silent week after week, afraid to open my mouth because I didn't know how.

One Tuesday night, I decided it was time. I told myself, "Tomorrow's the day." I walked in determined, heart pounding, ready to finally speak. But when it came to me, I froze. Shaking, sweating, completely silent. The next week, I tried again, but this time I prayed before I got there. I asked God to help me. When my turn came, my leg was bouncing, sweat pouring, and I barely got out the word, "Lord…" There was a long pause, and then I remembered reading about a deep-sea fish the day before. So I said, "Lord, I'm thankful for the fish they discovered…" That was it. Thirty seconds. But I prayed.

It wasn't polished. It wasn't impressive. But it was real. And that's where it started. Years later, I teach and talk about prayer, but I never forget that moment, the shaky, uncertain step of faith that broke the silence. Men, if you don't know how to pray, pray anyway. Don't fake it. Faith it. We don't need the right words. We don't need to sound strong. We just need to show up honestly and trust that the Spirit meets us in our weakness.

Too many of us are trying to obey Jesus without first connecting with Him. We're trying to do things for Him before learning how to be with Him. That's why we burn out. That's why we get frustrated. Because we're chasing the mission without the map. Jesus made it clear, abide first, then fruit comes. Connection first, then direction.

I've learned that prayer doesn't have to be long to be powerful. Sometimes it's as simple as calling His name. Yeshua HaMashiach, Jesus the Messiah. I whisper it, I think it, I carry it. It brings me back to the truth that I'm not in control, He is. That's where everything shifts. That's where obedience flows out of relationship, not pressure. That's where real leadership begins.

Shepherding Value

Authentic connection — A shepherd leads with strength when his relationship with God comes first, allowing obedience to flow naturally from abiding in Christ.

Reflect

1. Jesus calls you to abide before you obey—are you connecting with Him personally or just trying to follow commands without relationship?

2. The Spirit helps you in your weakness—what fear is holding you back from honest, simple prayer before God?

3. Connection comes before direction—how is your lack of connection affecting how you lead your family right now?

Live It Today

Pray one simple, honest sentence to God today without overthinking your words.

Personal Prayer

Lord, teach me to connect with You before I try to act for You. Help me pray with honesty and faith.

Reflective Verse

John 15:5 (ESV)
"I am the vine; you are the branches. Whoever abides in me and I in him, he it is that bears much fruit, for apart from me you can do nothing."

Day 45

Serving Isn't the Mission!

Luke 10:42 (ESV)
"But one thing is necessary. Mary has chosen the good portion, which will not be taken away from her."

There was a time I thought being busy for God was the goal. I filled my days with work, ministry, and good things that looked right on the outside. But somewhere in all that movement, I missed the point. I wasn't really with Jesus. I was doing things for Him, but not walking with Him. That realization hit me hard, because everything I thought was strength was actually pulling me away from the very thing that mattered most.

I've read the story of Mary and Martha many times, but one day it hit differently. Martha was serving, moving, doing what needed to be done. Mary was sitting, still, listening, fully present with Jesus. And He said she chose the better portion. That cut deep, because I've lived more like Martha than I care to admit. Not because I wanted to ignore Jesus, but because I thought serving Him was enough. I was doing good things, but I was missing Him.

The world rewards men who stay busy, who produce, who keep moving and never slow down. But God calls us to something harder, stillness, intimacy, clarity. That doesn't come from doing more; it comes from sitting with Him. I've said yes to things I should've said no to. I've let noise drown out truth. I've looked like I was leading well on the outside while drying up on the inside. That's not leadership. That's distraction dressed up as purpose.

I had to face the truth that I was chasing approval, not presence. I was trying to prove something instead of protecting my relationship with Christ. When that happens, your vision gets blurry. Not just from sin, but from busyness, expectations, and trying to keep up with everything around you. And when your vision is off, your leadership follows. You can't shepherd your family well if you can't see clearly.

Jesus isn't asking for more effort. He's calling for your attention. He's saying come sit, be still, and choose what actually lasts. When I slowed down and started choosing time with Him again, everything began to realign. Not perfectly, but intentionally. That's where strength is built. That's where peace returns. That's where a man learns to lead from presence instead of pressure.

Shepherding Value

Stillness — A shepherd gains spiritual clarity and strength by choosing time with Jesus first, allowing leadership to flow from presence instead of performance.

Reflect

1. Jesus calls you to choose the better portion—are you sitting with Him or replacing Him with activity?

2. God forms your heart in His presence—where has busyness begun to dry you out instead of drawing you in?

3. Clarity comes from abiding with Christ—how is your distraction affecting how you lead your family right now?

Live It Today

Set aside uninterrupted time today to sit quietly with Jesus before doing anything else.

Personal Prayer

Lord, slow me down and help me choose You first. Give me clarity, peace, and strength as I sit at Your feet.

Reflective Verse

Matthew 5:8 (ESV)
"Blessed are the pure in heart, for they shall see God."

Day 46

Why God Is Raising the Bar in Your Life?

Romans 12:2 (ESV)
"Do not be conformed to this world, but be transformed by the renewal of your mind, that by testing you may discern what is the will of God, what is good and acceptable and perfect."

There's been a quiet pressure sitting in my chest lately, not fear, not stress, but something deeper. It doesn't shout, it presses. Like God is saying, "I'm doing something in you. Don't get ahead of Me." And I've learned to recognize that now. But I'll be honest, five years ago, I wouldn't have listened. I would've acted, moved, forced something forward, thinking I was doing the right thing.

Every time I did that, I got in the way. God was working at a level I couldn't see, and I stepped in too early. What came from it? No fruit. Just frustration and confusion. Looking back, it's clear, I was trying to carry something God hadn't given me yet. He wasn't holding back. I just wasn't ready. God doesn't reveal deeper things to men whose character can't carry them. That's not punishment. That's grace.

That truth changed how I pray. I stopped asking for fast results and started asking God to grow me into the man who could handle what He was preparing. Not louder prayers, not bigger moves, just daily obedience. Small steps. Consistency. That's where transformation actually happens. That's where Romans 12:2 becomes real, not in hype, but in steady renewal.

That pressure you feel? It might not be anxiety. It might be God stretching you, raising the bar, calling you deeper. If you rush it, you miss it. If you stay steady, you grow into it. Leadership is formed there, not in comfort, but in trust. Not in control, but in surrender.

So now I pray differently: "God, raise the bar in me." Not for comfort, but for character. Not for speed, but for strength. Because the man God is building isn't formed in chaos, he's formed in stillness, in obedience, in walking step by step with Him. And when the time comes, I'll be ready, because I didn't get ahead of Him.

Shepherding Value

Spiritual growth — A shepherd develops strength and clarity by allowing God to build his character over time instead of rushing ahead of His process.

Reflect

1. God is raising the bar in your life—are you trusting His timing or trying to move ahead of what He is doing?

2. God grows your character before giving more—what is He trying to develop in you that you are resisting right now?

3. God prepares you before you lead—how is your impatience affecting how you lead your family today?

Live It Today

Take one small step of obedience today instead of trying to force a bigger outcome.

Personal Prayer

Lord, raise the bar in my life and grow my character to match it. Keep me in step with You and teach me to trust Your process.

Reflective Verse

Romans 12:2 (ESV)
"Do not be conformed to this world, but be transformed by the renewal of your mind, that by testing you may discern what is the will of God, what is good and acceptable and per

From MenOfTheShepherd.com
Why God Is Raising the Bar in Your Life? | April 2, 2025

Day 47

It's Time to Stop Debating and Start Obeying

John 2:5 (ESV)
"His mother said to the servants, 'Do whatever he tells you.'"

God has no problem managing His time. He created it. We're the ones constantly saying, "I don't have time," like it's something to be proud of. It's not. It's an excuse, and it's killing our leadership. You've got 24 hours, same as every other man. The issue isn't time. It's what we choose to do with it. I had to learn that, and it started years ago when I began paying attention to how men actually handle time and priorities.

I remember sitting at an event in the late '90s with Donald Trump and Tony Robbins. They talked about everything they were managing, but what stuck with me wasn't the scale, it was how they viewed time. Same amount, different decisions. That moment shifted something in me. From then on, I focused on managing two things: my time and my priorities. And I've seen it clearly, those two define everything, especially as a man trying to lead his family well.

If you're leading a family, you're shepherding. And shepherding requires obedience, daily. Faith, loyalty, and humility aren't automatic. You choose them. Faith is commitment when there's no clear path. Loyalty is following God, not your version of Him. Humility is coming to Him as a son, not as someone trying to stay in control. This isn't theory, it's lived out in the small decisions you make every day.

We complicate something simple. "I don't have time to pray." That's not true. You've got seconds, 86,400 of them every day. The issue isn't time. It's willingness. Prayer isn't performance, it's presence. And presence requires obedience. You don't need perfect words. Sometimes it's just saying, "Jesus, I love You," and meaning it.

At some point, you stop debating and start obeying. Stop waiting. Act on what God has already made clear. When I stopped making excuses and started choosing obedience in the small moments, things shifted. Not instantly, but consistently. That's where leadership is built. That's where your family sees it. That's where your walk with Christ becomes real.

Shepherding Value

Obedience — A shepherd builds credibility and spiritual authority by consistently obeying God in everyday moments, not just when it is convenient.

Reflect

1. Jesus calls you to obey, not delay—are you using time as an excuse instead of responding to what He has already made clear?

2. God is worthy of your first priority—where is your heart choosing other things over time with Him?

3. Obedience is meant to be lived daily—how is your delay affecting how you lead your family right now?

Live It Today

Take ten seconds today and say a simple, honest prayer to Jesus without hesitation.

Personal Prayer

Lord, help me stop making excuses and start obeying You without hesitation. Make me a man who follows You in every moment.

Reflective Verse

Luke 23:46 (ESV)
"Then Jesus, calling out with a loud voice, said, 'Father, into your hands I commit my spirit!' And having said this he breathed his last."

From MenOfTheShepherd.com
It's Time to Stop Debating and Start Obeying | April 3, 2025

Day 48

Wake Up and Reflect

Psalm 139:23–24 (ESV)
"Search me, O God, and know my heart! Try me and know my thoughts! And see if there be any grievous way in me, and lead me in the way everlasting!"

I'm up early, usually around 3:30 or 4:00 AM. That's my time with God. I reflect, pray, and get my heart right before the day starts. But I'll be honest, there are days I'm not on it. Days where I'm distracted, tired, or just flat spiritually. And that's when it hits me: I still have to show up. I don't get to clock out just because I feel off.

If you belong to Jesus, you don't get to drift through your day and then wonder why your home feels disconnected. Your wife needs you present. Your kids need you grounded. And God is calling you to be awake, not half-engaged, not distracted, but ready. Jesus said He comes at an hour you don't expect, and that shows up in real life, in conversations, decisions, tension, and moments you didn't plan. The question is, are you paying attention?

There have been too many days where I missed Him. Not because I didn't care, but because I was distracted, doing life, staying busy, moving through the day without stopping to notice where God was working. That's what reflection exposed in me. When I started slowing down and letting God walk through my day with me, I began to see what I was missing. Where I showed up, and where I didn't.

That's why reflection matters. It's not just a habit, it's preparation. When you pause and let God search your heart, your awareness sharpens. You stop reacting and start responding like a man who knows who he follows. Whether it's morning or night, it doesn't matter. What matters is that you make the time and stop pretending you don't have it.

This world isn't slowing down, and your leadership can't be passive. If you want to lead your family well, you need clarity, and that starts with letting God inspect you before you step into the day. That's where readiness is built. That's where strength comes from. And that's where a shepherd learns to lead with a clear heart and a steady hand.

Shepherding Value

Readiness — A shepherd leads well when he stays spiritually alert, allowing God to search his heart and prepare him to respond with clarity and strength.

Reflect

1. God searches your heart—are you allowing Him to examine you or just moving through your day distracted?

2. Jesus shows up in the moments you miss—where has your heart been coasting instead of staying aware of Him?

3. You are called to be ready—how is your lack of awareness affecting how you lead your family right now?

Live It Today

Set aside five minutes today to pause and ask God to search your heart before continuing your day.

Personal Prayer

Lord, search my heart and make me ready. Help me lead with clarity, presence, and strength.

Reflective Verse

Luke 12:40 (ESV)
"You also must be ready, for the Son of Man is coming at an hour you do not expect."

Day 49

It's Time to Surrender Like a Man

2 Corinthians 3:17 (ESV)
*"Now the Lord is the Spirit, and where the Spirit of the Lord is,
there is freedom."*

Brother, let me speak straight to you. Spiritual formation isn't about looking holy or having a clean checklist. It's not about pretending you've got it all together. It's about being shaped from the inside out to reflect Jesus. And that shaping doesn't start with effort, it starts with surrender. Real surrender. The kind that says, "Lord, Your will, not mine," even when it costs you control.

We carry too much. The pressure to lead perfectly, provide constantly, have every answer, and never break, it's crushing. And when we try to control all of it, we end up controlled by fear, pride, and shame. That's not strength. That's bondage. God never asked you to carry that weight. He's asking you to lay it down. Because freedom doesn't come from control, it comes from surrender.

When we actually mean "Thy will be done," not just in words but in how we live, something shifts. You step into a strength that doesn't depend on you holding everything together. It's steady, grounded, and real. It says, "I trust the One who is in control." That's the kind of strength your family needs, not perfection, but a man anchored in Christ and led by the Spirit.

I had to learn to stop chasing performance and start pursuing presence. That's where God does the real work. He breaks what needs to be broken, rebuilds what matters, and forms you into a man who can actually lead. Not for applause, not for approval, but for legacy. For your wife. For your kids. For what comes after you.

So stop measuring yourself against something God never asked of you. Let go of the pressure. Lay it down. Pick up the truth. Surrender isn't weakness, it's strength. The kind that lasts. The kind that leads. The kind that serves.

Shepherding Value

Surrender — A shepherd leads with lasting strength when he releases control to God and trusts Him to shape his life, his leadership, and his family.

Reflect

1. God calls you to surrender, not control—where is your heart still resisting His will?

2. True strength is found in laying it down—what pressure are you still carrying instead of giving to God?

3. Surrender shapes how you lead—how is your resistance or obedience affecting your family right now?

Live It Today

Surrender one specific area of control to God in prayer and release it fully.

Personal Prayer

Lord, help me let go of control and trust Your will. Build strength in me through surrender and lead my life Your way.

Reflective Verse

Isaiah 59:16 (ESV)
"He saw that there was no man, and wondered that there was no one to intercede; then his own arm brought him salvation, and his righteousness upheld him."

From MenOfTheShepherd.com
It's Time to Surrender Like a Man | April 7, 2025

Day 50

It's Time to Fight for Your Home

1 John 5:16 (ESV)
"If anyone sees his brother committing a sin not leading to death, he shall ask, and God will give him life…"

You want to do whatever you want, whenever you want. I get it, so do I. But freedom doesn't come from doing what we want. It comes from doing what's right. Commitment and discipline are what actually make us free. We've been sold a lie that strength comes without sacrifice. It doesn't. You won't lead your family well until you understand this: leadership begins on your knees.

I had to face that myself. It's easy to sit back and see what's wrong, in your home, in your family, and in the people around you. It's easy to point it out, talk about it, or shut down. But that's not leadership. That's distance. The moment God shows you something in someone else, especially in your family, you have a choice. You can criticize them and make it about you, or you can pray for them and make it about God.

That shift is everything. God doesn't give you discernment so you can feel right, He gives it so you can intercede. That's the role of a shepherd. That's the responsibility. When I stopped reacting and started praying, I realized how much I had been missing. I wasn't fighting for my family. I was observing them. And that's not what I'm called to do.

No one starts ready. You grow into this. Just like a child learns to walk, a man learns to lead step by step. One prayer. One moment. One decision at a time. You might feel like you've failed before. So have I. But that doesn't disqualify you. It calls you back. Your family doesn't need perfection. They need presence. They need to see you show up and lead, even if it's small.

This is where it becomes real. Jesus intercedes for you, and now you step into that role for your family. Not perfectly, but faithfully. You stop waiting, stop making excuses, and start fighting the right way. On your knees. In prayer. That's where leadership is built. That's where your home changes. That's where you become the shepherd God called you to be.

Shepherding Value

Intercession — A shepherd leads by bringing the needs, struggles, and sins of his family before God in prayer instead of reacting, criticizing, or withdrawing.

Reflect

1. Jesus intercedes for you—where are you choosing to react instead of bringing others before Him in prayer?

2. You are called to fight on your knees—what is your response revealing about your dependence on God or yourself?

3. Your family depends on your leadership—how can you model intercession instead of criticism in your home today?

Live It Today

Pray out loud for one person in your family today instead of staying silent.

Personal Prayer

Lord, teach me to fight for my family in prayer. Help me lead with strength, humility, and faith.

Reflective Verse

Hebrews 7:25 (ESV)
"Consequently, he is able to save to the uttermost those who draw near to God through him, since he always lives to make intercession for them."

Day 51

Take a Time Out!

Psalm 77:11 (ESV)
"I will remember the deeds of the Lord; yes, I will remember your wonders of old."

You're worn out because you're running hard, but not running with God. I had to face that in my own life. I was moving fast, handling responsibilities, trying to do what I thought was right, but something was off. My time with God wasn't real, it was rushed, distracted, secondary. I wasn't stopping to be with Him. I was doing "God's work" without walking with God, and it was showing up in everything.

Life kept pulling. Work, pressure, expectations, people depending on me. I told myself I was just busy, just trying to survive. But the truth hit me hard, life wasn't too busy, I just wasn't still. I was choosing everything else first. Prayer slipped. Worship became optional. And slowly, my heart started to change. I got short, distant, frustrated. Not because I didn't care, but because I was empty.

That's when I realized I was outpacing God. Doing good things, but not in step with the Spirit. I had to stop and admit it. The Holy Spirit wasn't distant, He was already in me, ready to lead, ready to bring peace. But I wasn't making space. So I called a time-out. I stopped everything, sat in silence, and remembered that Jesus wasn't far off, He was interceding for me. The Spirit was active, not passive. That truth hit deep.

But I wouldn't have felt any of it if I didn't stop. I had to stop rushing, stop pretending I had control, stop numbing the pressure. Worship wasn't about routine, it was about keeping my heart soft and my vision clear. Remembering what God has done changes everything. It shifts you from panic to peace, from striving to surrender.

If I want to lead my family with strength, it starts on my knees. If I want clarity, I have to seek His face first. Leadership doesn't come from skill, it comes from surrender. So I say His name, Jesus. I slow down. I remember. And I lead from His presence, not my pressure. That's where strength is rebuilt. That's where real leadership begins.

Shepherding Value

Stillness in God's presence strengthens your leadership at home.

Reflect

1. You're running hard but not running with God—are you actually walking with Jesus or just staying busy for Him?

2. You stopped being still and your heart started to harden—what pressure are you allowing to replace your time with God?

3. You became short and distant at home from running on empty—how is your lack of time with God affecting your family right now?

Live It Today

Set a 10-minute time-out today—no phone, no noise—sit still and speak the name of Jesus.

Personal Prayer

Father, slow me down. Teach me to lead from Your presence, not my pressure.

Reflective Verse

Psalm 46:10 (ESV)
"Be still, and know that I am God."

Day 52

Step Up and Lead Boldly

Matthew 11:29 (ESV)
"Take my yoke upon you, and learn from me, for I am gentle and lowly in heart, and you will find rest for your souls."

I spent way too many years trying to please people instead of pleasing God. I was always measuring myself against someone else, trying to be good enough, strong enough, respected enough. On the outside, it looked like effort and drive. But inside, it was pressure. I kept pushing forward, thinking that's what a man does. Handle it. Carry it. Figure it out. But the more I carried, the more exhausted I became, and the more I realized something wasn't right.

When I first came to faith, I didn't know what walking with Jesus actually looked like. I wanted direction. I wanted someone to show me how to lead my family in faith. But instead of clarity, I ran into expectations. Rules. Silence when I needed guidance. I remember reaching out when I felt called toward counseling, only to be met with nothing. Then when I moved forward anyway, I was labeled a "lone wolf." That moment stuck. It exposed something deeper, I was depending on people to tell me I was worthy instead of trusting God who already called me.

That was the turning point. I had to face it, my burden wasn't leadership, it was approval. I was carrying something Jesus never asked me to carry. And everything shifted the moment I surrendered that weight. On January 15, 2025, I stopped measuring myself by man's standards and trusted Christ's calling. I realized I don't become worthy by proving myself, I am worthy because He called me and walks beside me.

Men, Jesus is not asking you to carry more. He is asking you to come closer. His yoke is not pressure, it is presence. When you walk with Him, leadership stops being forced and starts flowing. Your family doesn't need a man striving under pressure. They need a man walking in step with Christ. Step up. Not by trying harder, but by surrendering deeper.

Shepherding Value

Surrendered Leadership — A shepherd leads with strength when he releases man's expectations and walks fully under Christ's direction.

Reflect

- You are carrying pressure to prove yourself—are you walking under Jesus' yoke or still trying to earn your worth?

- You have been seeking approval from others—what is that revealing about your trust in God's calling?

- Your family is watching your leadership—are you leading from pressure or from peace in Christ?

Live It Today

Identify one expectation you're carrying that didn't come from God and surrender it in prayer before leading your family today.

Personal Prayer

Jesus, take the weight I was never meant to carry. Teach me to walk with You and lead from Your strength.

Reflective Verse

Matthew 11:30 (ESV)
"For my yoke is easy, and my burden is light."

Day 53

Real Men Bleed Worship
Spiritual Grit Starts Here

Romans 5:3 (ESV)
"Not only that, but we rejoice in our sufferings, knowing that suffering produces endurance."

There are things I've walked through that should've broken me. Divorce. Financial ruin. Complete emotional collapse. There were days I didn't know where my next meal would come from. Everything was stripped down to nothing. But one thing never left me, my relationship with God. Not church. Not routines. Not feelings. Just God. And when everything else failed, that's what held.

I've stood beside people as a chaplain, watching grief rip through their lives. When death shows up, all the surface-level faith disappears. I've seen men blame God, walk away, or collapse because what they thought was faith couldn't survive pressure. It wasn't built on Jesus, it was built on comfort. And comfort doesn't hold when life hits hard. That's where the difference shows up.

What held me together wasn't anything I could manufacture. It wasn't effort or discipline or trying harder. It was Jesus. It was the Spirit reminding me I wasn't done. That's where spiritual grit was formed, not in strength, but in surrender. John 3:30 became real: He must increase, I must decrease. That's not theory. That's the breaking point where everything shifts.

I don't write this from a place of having it figured out. I write it from being broken and rebuilt. Spiritual grit is not built when life is easy, it's forged when everything falls apart and you still choose to trust Him. Like Job said, even if it all goes, hope in Him remains. That's the kind of faith your family needs to see. Not talk. Not noise. Real worship in the fire.

Shepherding Value

Spiritual Grit — A shepherd leads with strength when he remains rooted in Christ through pressure, pain, and uncertainty.

Reflect

1. You have walked through suffering—did it push you closer to Jesus or pull you away from Him?

2. You have faced pressure and pain—what does your response reveal about where your strength truly comes from?

3. Your family is watching your trials—are you showing them grit rooted in Christ or collapse under pressure?

Live It Today

When pressure hits today, stop and pray immediately instead of reacting—choose to lean into Christ instead of yourself.

Personal Prayer

Father, build real grit in me. Strip away my pride and anchor me in You when life gets hard.

Reflective Verse

2 Corinthians 12:9 (ESV)
"My grace is sufficient for you, for my power is made perfect in weakness."

Day 54

Be a Man – Pray Like One!

Hebrews 2:17 (ESV)
"Therefore he had to be made like his brothers in every respect, so that he might become a merciful and faithful high priest in the service of God, to make propitiation for the sins of the people."

Every man says he wants to lead his family well, but most aren't even praying for them. I had to face that myself. Prayer didn't come easy for me. I grew up with memorized words that sounded right but carried no weight. When I met Jesus, something changed. I wanted more than routine, I wanted something real. But wanting it and living it were two different things, and I had to learn how to actually step into prayer.

It wasn't natural. It took effort, repetition, and a decision to stay in it even when it felt awkward. I'm still learning. Because real prayer, the kind that carries your family before God, isn't casual. It's intentional. It's a man realizing that his leadership rises or falls on his connection with God. That realization forced a shift in me from passive words to purposeful prayer.

Jesus showed exactly what that looks like. In the garden, He didn't avoid the weight, He faced it. He wrestled with obedience and stayed in the presence of the Father. He didn't take a shortcut. He stepped into it fully as a man and prayed through it. That moment reframed everything for me. Prayer isn't performance, it's surrender under pressure.

That's where it changed. I stopped waiting to feel ready and started showing up. Saying His name. Speaking over my wife. Praying for my children. Not polished, not perfect, just consistent. That's where strength started to build. Not in what I could say, but in the fact that I stayed. That's the kind of leadership my family needs, a man who shows up before God and doesn't walk away.

Shepherding Value

Persistent Prayer: Real shepherding begins on your knees. Your family needs more than provision—they need your spiritual protection through consistent, intentional prayer.

Reflect

1. Jesus prayed under pressure and stayed in the fight—how does His example expose the way you approach prayer?

2. You say prayer matters—where have you avoided consistency, effort, or discipline in your walk with God?

3. Your family depends on your leadership—what would change in your home if you prayed over them daily with purpose?

Live It Today

Set a specific time today and pray intentionally over your wife, your children, and your leadership—out loud.

Personal Prayer

Lord, teach me to pray like a man who truly loves and leads. Strengthen my commitment to fight for my family through prayer every day.

Reflective Verse

Hebrews 4:15 (ESV)
"For we do not have a high priest who is unable to sympathize with our weaknesses, but one who in every respect has been tempted as we are, yet without sin."

Day 55

The Three Daggers of Self-Centeredness

Galatians 2:20 (ESV)
"I have been crucified with Christ. It is no longer I who live, but Christ who lives in me. And the life I now live in the flesh I live by faith in the Son of God, who loved me and gave himself for me."

This devotional didn't start deep. It started as a pet peeve. A rant. But the more I sat with it, the more it turned on me. It exposed something I couldn't ignore, how easy it is to speak in ways that sound spiritual but still revolve around self. I've seen it in others, but more importantly, I've had to see it in myself.

I've been around men in ministry, pastors, chaplains, leaders, who mean well, but everything circles back to "I," "me," and "my." At first, it sounds like confidence or experience. But over time, it reveals something deeper. Not leadership, performance. A man tuned into WIIFM, "What's In It For Me." And if I'm honest, I've had to check that same frequency in my own words.

That's where it hit me. These aren't just words. They can become daggers. The Three Daggers of Self-Centeredness. Not sinful on their own, but when they dominate, they shift the message. They pull attention off Jesus and redirect it toward the speaker. Even with good intentions, the focus drifts. It becomes more about the messenger than the One we're called to represent.

So I had to stop and ask the question that cuts through all of it: What's the object? Is it Jesus, or is it me? That question forces a decision. Because if my words, my leadership, or my influence point back to me, then I'm not shepherding, I'm showcasing. And that's not the man I'm called to be.

Jesus didn't live to promote Himself. He came to serve. He carried a cross, not a platform. That's the shift. My story matters, but it's not the point, it's the pointer. It must lead back to Him. So the decision is simple and hard at the same time: drop the daggers, pick up the cross, and lead by pointing everything back to Jesus.

Shepherding Value

Focus — A man who keeps Jesus at the center of his message leads with clarity, purpose, and strength that builds a Christ-honoring legacy.

Reflect

1. Jesus made Himself the servant and pointed everything to the Father—how does that challenge the way you speak about your faith?

2. Your words reveal what fills your heart—where are you still centered on yourself instead of Christ?

3. Your family listens to how you lead—how can you intentionally shift your words to point them toward Jesus more clearly?

Live It Today

Pay attention to your words in every conversation today and intentionally redirect them to reflect Jesus, not yourself.

Personal Prayer

Lord, strip my words of pride. Let me speak in a way that reflects You, not me. Let my life and leadership point only to the Cross.

Reflective Verse

Luke 9:23 (ESV)
"And he said to all, 'If anyone would come after me, let him deny himself and take up his cross daily and follow me.'"

Day 56

It's Time to Climb the Mountain

Romans 8:28 (ESV)
"And we know that for those who love God all things work together for good, for those who are called according to his purpose."

Ever feel like someone completely misunderstood your heart, and blasted you for it? That happened to me this week. I was blindsided. A man, full of pride and accusations, came hard at me and said I was acting without compassion. He was wrong, but he was loud. And in that moment, the Holy Spirit told me to stay quiet. As he spoke, I prayed, nothing polished, just "Yeshua HaMashiach." Because I knew something deeper was happening. Pride doesn't listen. It assumes. It attacks. And if I'm honest, I was hurt.

It would have been easy to defend myself or walk away. But instead, I kept praying. Step by step, like climbing a mountain I didn't ask for. And something began to change, not in him, but in me. That's when it hit me: leadership doesn't start with strategy, it starts with surrender. Until the Holy Spirit transforms what's inside, we can't lead clearly or love well. We try to guide others while still walking in our own fog.

Too many of us skip this. We rush to act and serve without letting God work on us first. We want outward impact without inward transformation. But that's backwards. It starts inside, then intimacy with Jesus, then serving others. This week forced me to face being misunderstood, but instead of fighting, I stayed in prayer and let God work.

I didn't call it a problem. I called it a challenge. A challenge means you're equipped and not climbing alone. With every prayer, I took another step. It wasn't easy, but as I kept climbing, I sensed Jesus with me, leading, strengthening, giving perspective and peace.

Men, it's time to climb. Lay down your pride. Stop trying to win. Start praying. Let the Holy Spirit change you from the inside. When He does, everything changes. You'll love better. You'll lead clearer. You'll shepherd with His strength. Put on your gear, and climb.

Shepherding Value

Inner Surrender — When a man lays down his pride and climbs toward God, he leads not from emotion but from transformation. That's real shepherding.

Reflect

1. You were told to stay quiet—are you listening to the Holy Spirit or reacting from pride?

2. You felt hurt and misunderstood—what does that reveal about your heart?

3. You kept climbing through prayer—how are you leading your family under pressure?

Live It Today

Pause and pray before your next response—choose surrender over reaction.

Personal Prayer

Lord, remove my pride and transform my heart so I can lead Your way.

Reflective Verse

Luke 10:27 (ESV)
"And he answered, 'You shall love the Lord your God with all your heart and with all your soul and with all your strength and with all your mind, and your neighbor as yourself.'"

Day 57

Pray Like a Shepherd

Romans 8:26 (ESV)
"Likewise the Spirit helps us in our weakness. For we do not know what to pray for as we ought, but the Spirit himself intercedes for us with groanings too deep for words."

It used to be that I prayed once or twice a day, and even that felt like progress compared to before. Back then, prayer was occasional, usually prompted by someone else, and almost always for other people. I never even thought about praying for myself. I didn't believe I was worthy. I saw my role as serving, protecting, providing, but somehow convinced myself that bringing my own needs to God was selfish.

Over time, something began to shift. It wasn't one moment, but a slow change through hardship, raising children, and stepping into the responsibility of shepherding my family. My prayer life deepened. It became more focused and more personal. I began to realize how much I needed Jesus, not just as Savior, but as Friend and guide. I stopped limiting my prayers to others and finally started praying for myself, not out of pride, but out of dependence.

The real issue had been shame. I thought I was being humble by staying silent about my own needs, but I was carrying a weight that didn't belong to me. I was thinking like a man trying to prove something, not like a son who had already been accepted. I let the world define my worth, forgetting that Jesus had already settled that at the cross. If He gave His life for me, then I am not disqualified from speaking His name.

If you're leading your family, you need to understand this: praying for yourself is not optional. When you pray for yourself, you are strengthening the man your family depends on. You are bringing your weakness, your fear, your exhaustion before God so He can meet you in it. That is not selfish, that is leadership. That is how you love your family well.

You are not meant to do this alone. The Holy Spirit was given to guide you, strengthen you, and draw you back to Jesus when everything in you wants control. You need that power, and you need to ask for it. You are worthy to pray, not because you earned it, but because Jesus paid for it. So pray. Out loud. With boldness. You are a man of the Shepherd, and you fight differently now.

Shepherding Value

Courage to Ask – A shepherd-leader must be brave enough to come before God for strength. Prayer is the front line of spiritual leadership.

Reflect

1. You avoided praying for yourself—are you trusting Jesus or still believing you are unworthy to come to Him?

2. You carried shame instead of dependence—what is keeping you silent before God right now?

3. You are called to lead your family—how does your lack of prayer affect the way you show up for them?

Live It Today

Pray out loud for yourself today, asking God for strength and guidance before you lead or act.

Personal Prayer

God, teach me to come to You boldly and depend on Your strength to lead my family well.

Reflective Verse

Luke 10:27 (ESV)
"And he answered, 'You shall love the Lord your God with all your heart and with all your soul and with all your strength and with all your mind, and your neighbor as yourself.'"

Day 58

Pick Up Your Sword, You Family Needs You – NOW!

Ezekiel 22:30 (ESV)
"And I sought for a man among them who should build up the wall and stand in the breach before me for the land, that I should not destroy it, but I found none."

When we go into battle, we don't go for ourselves, we go for our families. We carry the unseen weight, making sacrifices no one applauds. One of the greatest is prayer. Sometimes it's a whisper, sometimes tears, sometimes a battle cry, but every word matters. Your prayer is your sword, rooted in the Word and carried in faith. However you bring it, quiet, loud, short, or broken, bring it. Your family needs it.

It took me a long time to understand that prayer wasn't just for them, it was for me. I used to think I wasn't doing it right. I'd hear others pray with long, powerful words, covering everything, and I felt like I fell short. My mind wandered. My words were simple. I thought I was failing. But I learned something that changed everything: my prayers aren't supposed to sound like theirs. They're supposed to sound like me. My Father hears my voice.

Early on, I chased other men's prayer styles. One was intense, another organized with lists. I even found out one wrote everything down. That helped, but it also showed me something. I was trying to copy instead of connect. Over time, I stopped comparing and started praying honestly. That shift didn't happen overnight. It took years. But it grounded me. It made my prayer life real, not forced.

You and I are called to pray for our families. No exceptions. Whether it's in the morning, in the car, or in silence, your voice matters before God. When you start worrying if your prayer is good enough, you've already lost focus. You're looking at yourself instead of Him. God already knows your heart. He's not measuring your words, He's listening for your dependence.

You are in a war. Your family depends on your leadership. If you can speak their names to God, you can fight for them. Your sword isn't measured by how long you swing it, it's measured by how often you pick it up. So stop comparing. Stop holding back. Pray. Pray consistently. Pray faithfully. Pick up your sword, and fight for your family.

Shepherding Value

Consistency in prayer sharpens your role as a spiritual protector and steady leader for your family.

Reflect

1. You compared your prayers to others—are you focusing on God or measuring yourself?

2. You felt like your prayers weren't enough—what belief is keeping you from praying freely?

3. You are called to protect your family—how consistent is your prayer life for them right now?

Live It Today

Set one specific time today to pray for your family, even if it's brief—just be consistent.

Personal Prayer

Lord, teach me to pray with faith and consistency so I can lead and protect my family.

Reflective Verse

Romans 8:26 (ESV)
"Likewise the Spirit helps us in our weakness. For we do not know what to pray for as we ought, but the Spirit himself intercedes for us with groanings too deep for words."

Day 59

Kill Sin!

Romans 6:1–2 (ESV)
"What shall we say then? Are we to continue in sin that grace may abound? By no means! How can we who died to sin still live in it?"

When a man finally decides to kill the sin in his life, everything changes. This isn't about trying harder or cleaning things up on the surface. It's a line in the sand before God where you say, "Sin dies here." Because sin doesn't fade quietly. It doesn't loosen its grip just because you want it to. You can't manage it, ignore it, or keep it on a leash. Scripture is clear, you must crucify it. Put it to death.

That decision is the turning point. The moment you stop letting sin make decisions for you. The moment you realize your passivity, your anger, your addiction, or your silence is not just affecting you, it's dragging your family with you. Sin keeps you stuck in the mire, like Psalm 69 describes, where there is no foothold and everything pulls you under. And yet, Jesus offers a way out, but it starts at the cross.

This is personal. It's not about anyone else. It's about you standing before God and asking the hard question: have you decided that sin must die in you? Not later. Not eventually. Now. Because suppressing sin is not killing it. What you bury alive will keep breathing, keep stirring, and keep destroying. You can't fix what you refuse to face.

Take time alone with God. Let Him search your heart and expose what's hidden. Name the sin. Bring it into the light. Then bring it to the cross. This is where surrender happens. This is where Jesus takes over. "He must increase, but I must decrease." That's not theory, that's the fight. You die to sin so Christ can live in you.

And don't miss this, this isn't just about you. This is about your family. You cannot lead what you are still dragging through the mud. The sword of the Spirit is in your hand, but it means nothing if you won't use it. Decide today. Kill sin so Christ can live. That's where real leadership begins.

Shepherding Value

Radical surrender to Jesus clears the way for strong, godly leadership in your home.

Reflect

1. You know sin must die—are you surrendering it to Jesus or still holding onto it?

2. You have been suppressing sin—what are you refusing to fully face before God?

3. You are called to lead your family—how is your sin affecting them right now?

Live It Today

Identify one sin and bring it before God in full honesty—commit to putting it to death today.

Personal Prayer

Lord, expose the sin in me and give me the strength to crucify it so You can live fully in me.

Reflective Verse

Galatians 2:20 (ESV)
"I have been crucified with Christ. It is no longer I who live, but Christ who lives in me. And the life I now live in the flesh I live by faith in the Son of God, who loved me and gave himself for me."

Day 60

A Knight of A New Order

John 21:17 (ESV)
"He said to him the third time, 'Simon, son of John, do you love me?' Peter was grieved because he said to him the third time, 'Do you love me?' and he said to him, 'Lord, you know everything; you know that I love you.' Jesus said to him, 'Feed my sheep.'"

Wouldn't it be foolish to work hard, buy a house, and only take care of one room while the rest falls apart? Yet that's how too many men live spiritually. One area looks fine, but the rest is neglected. The foundation cracks, the roof leaks, and the damage spreads, but as long as something looks good, it's ignored. That's not leadership. That's avoidance.

When you pick up the sword, your house becomes your responsibility. Not just provision or maintenance, but people. Your home is your first church. Your wife, your children, and your own heart are all part of what you've been entrusted to lead. This is where shepherding begins. Not in a building, but in the place you live every day.

When Jesus asked Peter, "Do you love me?" He wasn't looking for words, He gave commands. Feed. Tend. Lead. That call wasn't about emotion. It was about responsibility. The same call stands now. Love for Christ is proven through how you lead what He placed in your care. Passive faith doesn't build anything. It leaves things exposed.

Too many men stay quiet, delay action, or wait until they feel ready. But this calling doesn't wait. You've been given what you need. The Word is your sword. Prayer connects you to the King. The mission is already clear. You don't create it, you step into it. This isn't about becoming something new later. It's about living what you've already been called into now.

You don't carry this alone, but you do carry it. Your house doesn't need perfection. It needs presence. It needs a man who will step forward, take responsibility, and lead with conviction. Pick up the sword. Tend the sheep. Lead your home with faithfulness and obedience.

Shepherding Value

Faithful responsibility. A shepherd-leader doesn't wait until he feels worthy—he obeys because God has already made him ready.

Reflect

1. When you say you love Jesus—how are you actively feeding and leading what He placed in your care?

2. That area of your life you've neglected—what are you avoiding taking responsibility for?

3. In your home right now—where do you need to step up and lead instead of waiting?

Live It Today

Choose one area of your home and take clear responsibility for it today—act, don't delay.

Personal Prayer

Lord, help me take full responsibility for my home and lead with faith and obedience.

Reflective Verse

Matthew 28:19 (ESV)
"Go therefore and make disciples of all nations, baptizing them in the name of the Father and of the Son and of the Holy Spirit."

Day 61

Absolute Dominion

Romans 6:9–11 (ESV)
"We know that Christ, being raised from the dead, will never die again; death no longer has dominion over him. For the death he died he died to sin, once for all, but the life he lives he lives to God. So you also must consider yourselves dead to sin and alive to God in Christ Jesus."

Jesus didn't partially die on the cross. He gave everything. Because He truly died, He now fully lives, and we are called to live the same way: dead to sin and alive to God. But too many men try to hold both. They talk about leading with Christ's strength while still gripping control, opinions, and emotions. That isn't leadership. That's self-deception. You can't carry the cross in one hand and your ego in the other.

There is no such thing as partial surrender. Jesus has absolute dominion, over death, over sin, over every part of your life. The Holy Spirit is not given in pieces. He is the power. And if He's not in control, then you are. That's where the breakdown happens. Men pray and then panic. They pray and then step in like God needs help. That's not faith. That's fear dressed up as obedience.

Look at how Jesus moved. Before calling Lazarus out of the grave, He paused and prayed. Then He acted. That's the order: pause, pray, proceed. Connection before command. That's how a shepherd leads, by following first. Power doesn't come from effort. It comes from surrender. You don't get filled with God while holding onto yourself. You have to be emptied first.

Every man reaches the same decision point: hold on or hand it over. You can keep trying to control your home, your family, your life, or you can surrender it to the One who already conquered death. This isn't weakness. This is strength. Kneel first. Wait with confidence. Then move in obedience like your prayer is already answered.

Stop asking for power while holding onto control. Stop pretending to wait on God when your mind is already made up. Die to yourself fully. Then you will understand what it means to be alive in Christ. Let Jesus take dominion.

Shepherding Value

Obedience before movement gives birth to power. When a man kneels first, he rises ready to lead.

Reflect

1. When you pray but still hold control—are you truly trusting Jesus or managing outcomes yourself?

2. That place where you panic after praying—what fear is still driving your decisions?

3. In your leadership at home—where do you need to pause, pray, and then proceed instead of reacting?

Live It Today

Pause before your next decision, pray first, then act in obedience without taking control back.

Personal Prayer

Father, help me release control and trust You fully so I can lead with Your power, not mine.

Reflective Verse

John 11:41–42 (ESV)
"So they took away the stone. And Jesus lifted up his eyes and said, 'Father, I thank you that you have heard me. I knew that you always hear me…'"

Day 62

The Wonderful Burden

Matthew 11:28 (ESV)
"Come to me, all who labor and are heavy laden, and I will give you rest."

Being a man of God is not easy, and it's not supposed to be. Leading your home, raising children, standing in the gap, this is where the weight shows up. But it's a wonderful burden. Not because it starts light, but because when it's carried with Jesus, it becomes something different. Years ago, I was raising my kids alone, newly divorced, barely making enough, and trying to figure out how to lead. It was heavy, lonely, and uncertain, and I knew I wasn't built to carry it all myself.

Some of you are there right now. Pressure stacking up, expectations rising, and no clear relief in sight. You're trying to do what's right, but doing it alone is exactly how men break. Jesus didn't say, "Figure it out." He said, "Come to Me." Not when everything is fixed, but in the middle of the mess. When I stopped trying to be the one holding everything together and let Him lead, things began to shift. Not perfectly, but steadily. Peace started replacing panic.

We prayed. We stayed in the Word as best we could. It wasn't polished, but it was real. And over time, Jesus carried what I couldn't. He didn't remove every problem, but He walked with me through them. Looking back now, I see the fruit. My kids love Jesus. They follow Him. That didn't come from perfection, it came from dependence. God honored those early, unsteady steps.

There were nights I felt like I was sinking. Moments where I didn't think I had anything left. But every time I took my eyes off Jesus, I felt it immediately. And every time I cried out, He was there. That's the pattern. Walk, stumble, refocus, repeat. The burden never disappeared, but it was never mine to carry alone.

The weight isn't the problem. Carrying it without God is. When you place it on Him, you don't lose responsibility, you gain strength. You stand beside Him instead of under it. This is the call: don't run from the burden. Don't pretend it's light. Carry it with Jesus. Because with Him, even the heaviest load becomes something you can bear, and something that produces life.

Shepherding Value

Surrendered Strength — Real Biblical leadership begins when a man stops relying on himself and fully depends on Christ. That surrender is what strengthens a shepherd to lead his family well.

Reflect

1. When you try to carry everything alone—are you coming to Jesus or relying on your own strength?

2. That weight you feel right now—what are you refusing to surrender to God?

3. In your role at home—how would your leadership change if you depended on Christ instead of yourself?

Live It Today

Give one burden to God in prayer and consciously release control over it today.

Personal Prayer

Lord, I release this weight to You and ask for strength to lead with You, not apart from You.

Reflective Verse

1 Peter 5:7 (ESV)
"Casting all your anxieties on him, because he cares for you."

Day 63

Dedicated Discipleship

John 17:17 (ESV)
"Sanctify them in the truth; your word is truth."

We are not meant to drift through manhood. We are called to be sanctified, set apart, different, devoted. And that starts with truth. Jesus didn't ask the Father to simply improve us. He asked Him to set us apart for something higher. That includes every man who claims to follow Him. Not perfect men. Not polished men. But men willing to be shaped by truth instead of the world.

The world has lied about what strength looks like. It says dominate, succeed, stand alone. But real strength is found in surrender. In letting God define you, not culture. Sanctification is not surface-level change, it's deep transformation. God takes your life, with all its flaws and failures, and calls it into purpose. Not because you earned it, but because He set you apart.

Jesus set Himself apart so you could be set apart. That wasn't for comfort. It was for mission. You are not in a war against people, you are in a war for your soul and your family. And if you follow the world's definition of manhood, you will lose both. Truth is what anchors you. Truth is what guides your leadership. Without it, everything drifts.

You want to lead your home well? Then lead in truth. You want to strengthen your family? Then live it out daily. Joy is not optional in that process, it is strength. When pressure hits, joy holds the line. Not fake emotion, but confidence in who God is and what He has done in you. That's what keeps a man steady.

You may feel worn down or behind. That doesn't disqualify you. You have been washed, sanctified, and set apart already. Now walk like it. Your legacy won't come from trying harder, it will come from living surrendered. Be different. Be steady. Be a man set apart in truth.

Shepherding Value

Sanctification through Truth — A shepherd leads best when he lives set apart, grounded in God's Word, and marked by the joy of the Lord.

Reflect

1. When you follow the world's definition of strength—are you surrendering to truth or chasing control?

2. That area where you feel worn down—what truth from God's Word are you ignoring?

3. In your home—how are you showing your family what it means to live set apart?

Live It Today

Choose one truth from Scripture and intentionally live it out in your home today.

Personal Prayer

Father, set me apart in Your truth and help me lead my home with strength and joy.

Reflective Verse

Nehemiah 8:10 (ESV)
"…And do not be grieved, for the joy of the Lord is your strength."

Day 64

Right Takes Time

Colossians 3:23 (ESV)
"Whatever you do, work heartily, as for the Lord and not for men."

I hear it all the time after someone dies: "He was a good man." "He went to church." "He was right with God." But what does that really mean? That question hits deeper than we want it to. Because it forces a hard look, am I actually living for Jesus, or have I settled into doing good things for the wrong reasons? It's easy to build a rhythm that looks right on the outside while pride quietly runs the show underneath.

For me, that's where it exposed itself, pride. I can look back and see seasons where I thought I was doing the Lord's work. And in part, I was. But the truth is, I wanted something from it. Recognition. Approval. A sense of being seen. Even in moments that could have honored God, the spotlight was still tilted toward me. That's not shepherding. That's self-promotion dressed up in service.

We are called to lead, but we are still under authority. Knights of the Shepherd, yes, but still sheep. That means our focus can't drift to applause, titles, or results. It has to stay locked on Jesus. That's harder than it sounds. Because everything around us feeds pride, success, attention, validation. And if we're not careful, we start serving those things instead of God.

This is not a quick fix. Obedience takes time. It's a daily grind of checking your heart, adjusting your focus, and choosing the right direction again and again. The question is simple, but it cuts deep: is what you're doing bringing glory to God, or to you? The task doesn't matter as much as the focus behind it.

When your focus shifts to Jesus, everything changes. Work becomes worship. Quiet sacrifice becomes meaningful. Even the things no one sees matter. Because He sees them. And He's the one you answer to. So check your mission. Put your pride down. Lift your eyes up. Let your life point to Him, not you.

Shepherding Value

Focus — When we focus on Jesus, our work, our roles, and our leadership become acts of worship that reflect our true calling as shepherds.

Reflect

1. When you do good things—are you working for Jesus or for how others see you?

2. That area where pride shows up—what is it revealing about what you really want?

3. In your daily leadership—how can you shift your focus so your family sees Christ instead of you?

Live It Today

Choose one task today and intentionally do it for Jesus alone, not for recognition.

Personal Prayer

Father, expose my pride and help me live in a way that gives You the glory, not me.

Reflective Verse

Matthew 6:1 (ESV)
"Beware of practicing your righteousness before other people in order to be seen by them…"

Day 65

Guard Your Home!

1 Peter 5:8 (ESV)
"Be sober-minded; be watchful. Your adversary the devil prowls around like a roaring lion, seeking someone to devour."

When I first came to Christ, I was hungry. I wanted everything, truth, growth, direction. I leaned on pastors, elders, and other believers to guide me, assuming anyone who spoke the name of Jesus was pointing me the right way. But I wasn't standing guard. I didn't realize that hunger without vigilance leaves you exposed. And the enemy knew exactly where to press, through pride, confusion, and half-truths.

I wasn't alert. I didn't keep my sword ready. I trusted too quickly and watched too little. That's where the cracks started. And here's the truth: the enemy doesn't wait for your lowest moment. He prowls when you're strong, when you're growing, when you're stepping forward. He looks for openings. And if you're not watchful, those openings grow right under your feet.

Vigilance is not optional for a man of God. It's part of the calling. It's standing guard over your wife, your children, and your own heart. It's refusing to let spiritual drift creep in while you get distracted or passive. This isn't about fear, it's about active faith. It's picking up your sword daily and staying ready. The enemy may prowl, but he's already defeated. The power of the Holy Spirit stands stronger than anything he brings.

But that power doesn't operate through passivity. It requires action. Staying alert. Moving intentionally. Correcting quickly when you drift. When pride shows up, deal with it. When complacency creeps in, confront it. You don't wait, you respond. That's how you protect what God entrusted to you.

A passive man doesn't just hurt himself, he leaves his home exposed. That's the weight of this calling. You cannot drift into faithful leadership. You choose it, again and again. So pick up your sword. Stand your ground. Guard your home. Lead your family under the authority of Jesus, and don't step back into passivity again.

Shepherding Value

Spiritual Vigilance — Guarding your home with alertness, intentional action, and quick correction strengthens your leadership as a faithful shepherd over your family.

Reflect

1. When you rely on others without discernment—are you staying watchful or leaving yourself open?

2. That area where you've grown passive—what have you allowed to creep in unnoticed?

3. In your home leadership—how are you actively standing guard over your family right now?

Live It Today

Take one intentional step today to guard your home—read Scripture, pray out loud, and address one area of drift.

Personal Prayer

Father, sharpen my awareness and give me the strength to guard what You've entrusted to me.

Reflective Verse

Hebrews 4:12 (ESV)
"For the word of God is living and active, sharper than any two-edged sword…"

Day 66

Ready! Willing! Able!

Colossians 3:23 (ESV)
"Whatever you do, work heartily, as for the Lord and not for men."

There was a time when I was unemployed, back in the 80s and 90s, standing in lines and answering the same question over and over: "Are you ready, willing, and able to work?" Back then it felt routine, but now I see it differently. When it comes to following Jesus, that question doesn't go away. It gets deeper. Are you ready to lead? Willing to surrender? Able to obey when it's hard, unseen, or uncomfortable?

I thought I was. I went to church, prayed, and believed I had a relationship with God. But looking back, it was surface-level. It was real, but shallow. Now it feels different, like a fire that won't go out. And that fire exposed something: I wasn't as ready as I thought. I said yes to God, but only in the areas that didn't cost me much. When obedience stepped into discomfort, I hesitated. I stalled. I tried to reshape what He was asking.

Surrender is not a one-time moment. It's a daily battle. I've prayed, "Jesus, take it all," and then quietly held parts back. I've given up control, then grabbed it again the moment things felt uncertain. And obedience? That's where it hits hardest. Not because it's complicated, but because it demands something from you, your pride, your comfort, your plans.

What I'm learning is this: God isn't measuring perfection. He's looking at the heart. Do you want Him more than your own way? Do you desire to follow, even when you stumble? That desire matters. That's where transformation starts. Not in doing everything right, but in giving Him everything you are.

So the question remains: are you ready, willing, and able? Not in your own strength, but because Christ makes you able. This isn't about waiting for the perfect moment. It's about stepping forward now, leading your home, loving your family, and obeying the call in front of you. Be ready. Be willing. Be obedient.

Shepherding Value

Readiness — A true shepherd leader doesn't wait for the spotlight; he shows up, steps in, and stays alert to God's call, wherever it comes.

Reflect

1. When God prompts you to act—are you stepping forward or hesitating for a better moment?

2. That place where you keep taking control back—what are you unwilling to fully surrender?

3. In your home leadership—where do you need to act now instead of waiting for comfort?

Live It Today

Take one clear step of obedience today, even if it feels small or uncomfortable.

Personal Prayer

Father, make me ready when You call, willing when it costs, and obedient in every step.

Reflective Verse

James 1:22 (ESV)
"But be doers of the word, and not hearers only, deceiving yourselves."

Day 67

Are You Doing the Right Thing… the Right Way?

Colossians 3:23 (ESV)
"Whatever you do, work heartily, as for the Lord and not for men."

As men are called to lead, we have to stop and ask hard questions. We must ask not just whether we are doing enough, but whether we are doing the right things and doing them the right way. That kind of evaluation is not weakness, it is leadership. It is stewardship. It is obedience. And it forces us to look beyond routine and into purpose.

Over the past months, I committed to posting devotionals five days a week. It was consistent, structured, and meaningful work. But after stepping back, looking at the results, and spending time in prayer, something became clear. Not every effort was bearing fruit. Some days showed strong engagement. Others didn't. Continuing out of habit would have been easy, but it would not have been faithful.

That realization forced a decision. Not to quit, but to refine. To shift from five days to three, Sunday, Wednesday, and Thursday. Not because the work mattered less, but because it mattered more. Time is limited. Energy is not endless. And if this calling is going to remain strong, it has to be stewarded well. That means choosing depth over volume and impact over routine.

This is not just about a schedule. It is about alignment. Leadership requires the willingness to pause, evaluate, and adjust. Too many men keep pushing forward in areas that no longer produce anything meaningful. They stay busy but miss the point. Real shepherding requires awareness, knowing when to press forward and when to recalibrate.

So the question turns outward. Where are you investing time that no longer produces fruit? What needs to be cut back so something stronger can grow? This is not about doing less. It is about doing what matters most, with clarity and purpose. Lead with intention. Adjust when needed. Stay faithful to the mission, not the habit.

Shepherding Value

Intentional Stewardship — A shepherd-leader evaluates his actions, adjusts his focus, and commits to what produces lasting fruit.

Reflect

1. When you stay busy out of habit—are you following God's direction or avoiding hard evaluation?

2. That area where effort isn't producing fruit—what are you resisting changing?

3. In your leadership at home—where do you need to adjust your focus to better serve your family?

Live It Today

Identify one area of wasted effort and redirect that time toward something that produces real impact.

Personal Prayer

Father, give me clarity to see what matters and courage to adjust where needed.

Reflective Verse

John 15:2 (ESV)
"Every branch in me that does not bear fruit he takes away, and every branch that does bear fruit he prunes, that it may bear more fruit."

Day 68

Kill the Excuses!

2 Corinthians 7:1 (ESV)
"Since we have these promises, beloved, let us cleanse ourselves from every defilement of body and spirit, bringing holiness to completion in the fear of God."

Holiness is not a Sunday concept, it is the foundation of real manhood. And I'm not talking about a movement, a denomination, or some religious label. I'm talking about a life set apart for Jesus. God's commands are not there to restrict you, but to make you whole. A man walking in holiness is steady, grounded, and alive in truth. But the danger shows up when you assume the battles you once won no longer need guarding. That mindset opens the door, and the enemy moves quietly through comfort, distraction, and pride.

I have seen it in my own life and in the lives of men who should have known better. Strength becomes the very place of failure when it goes unguarded. The same areas where confidence grows are the same areas where compromise begins if vigilance fades. It is easy to think past victories guarantee present strength. They do not. What matters is today. Right now. Whether you are walking closely with Jesus or drifting while pretending nothing has changed.

Holiness is not about perfection. It is about pursuit. It is steady, intentional progress, daily decisions that move you closer to Christ. Not occasional effort, but consistent obedience. Not performance, but direction. When you truly love God, you stop asking how much you can get away with. You start asking how much closer you can get. That shift changes everything.

There are moments when the weight of sin, pride, or failure becomes obvious. That is not the time to retreat, it is the time to respond. When you stumble, you look up, not down. Jesus meets you there, not with condemnation, but with power to move forward. That is where growth happens. Not in pretending, but in confronting and continuing.

A man who walks in holiness becomes a man worth following. His strength is not in appearance, but in consistency. He leads his home with clarity, purpose, and conviction. This is not easy, and it is not quick. But it is the path. Kill the excuses. Guard your walk. Choose obedience today.

Shepherding Value

Daily obedience strengthens a man's spiritual foundation and leads his family with steady, unwavering purpose.

Reflect

1. When you rely on past victories—are you staying vigilant or assuming you are safe?

2. That area where you feel strong—what have you stopped guarding in your daily walk?

3. In your home leadership—how are you modeling consistent obedience instead of occasional effort?

Live It Today

Choose one area of your life and intentionally practice obedience in it today, without delay.

Personal Prayer

Father, expose my weak spots and strengthen me to walk in holiness with consistency and truth.

Reflective Verse

Matthew 22:37 (ESV)
"You shall love the Lord your God with all your heart and with all your soul and with all your mind."

Day 69

Breakthrough!

2 Corinthians 9:8 (ESV)
"And God is able to make all grace abound to you, so that having all sufficiency in all things at all times, you may abound in every good work."

It hit me hard. A couple of men I respected came at me with emotion, pride, and assumptions. They asked questions, but they were not listening. For almost an hour, they pressed in, accusing and attacking. I sat there, praying silently, not for escape, but asking God to keep me from becoming reactionary, defensive, or prideful. That moment became my battlefield.

For weeks after, it stayed with me. My thoughts ran, sleep was gone, and I looked for someone to talk to, someone to affirm my side. No one was available. Not for hours, for days. And in that silence, God did something deeper. He did not give comfort. He gave clarity. That moment was not about them, it was about me. How I would respond under pressure revealed what was actually leading me.

I had read the truth before: if God calls you, He equips you. But I missed it in practice. I started questioning. I let anxiety take over. Pride whispered that I should not have to go through this. In that moment, I limited the Spirit by trying to operate in my own strength. That is not leadership. That is immaturity. Real strength is trusting God's righteousness, not leaning on your own.

God does not promise ease. He promises sufficiency. If you have the Holy Spirit, you are already equipped. Not partially, fully. The problem is not what you lack. It is what you refuse to use. When pressure comes, you are not called to collapse. You are called to stand, pray, and respond with conviction instead of emotion.

Breakthrough is not a moment of relief. It is a decision to trust God in the middle of the fire. It is choosing obedience when everything in you wants to react. It is leading your home with confidence, not because things are calm, but because Christ is in control. Pick up your sword. Stand firm. Lead with what you have already been given.

Shepherding Value

Trusting God's Provision as you lead, even when you feel attacked, alone, or unqualified.

Reflect

1. When you are under pressure—are you responding in the Spirit or reacting from emotion?

2. That moment when you felt alone—what did it reveal about where you place your trust?

3. In your leadership at home—how can you stand firm instead of pulling back when things get hard?

Live It Today

Choose one situation today and respond with prayer and conviction before speaking or acting.

Personal Prayer

Lord, help me trust Your provision and lead with strength and clarity, even when I feel attacked or alone.

Reflective Verse

Matthew 6:33 (ESV)
"But seek first the kingdom of God and his righteousness, and all these things will be added to you."

From MenOfTheShepherd.com
Breakthrough! | May 7, 2025

Day 70

Are You Hurting Jesus?

John 14:1 (ESV)
"Let not your hearts be troubled. Believe in God; believe also in me."

I'm going to speak straight, brother to brother. You want to lead your home well. You love God. You want to be a steady husband and a present father. But you're tired, anxious, and carrying thoughts you were never meant to carry. I know that because I do it too. My wife tells me I think too much, and she's right. I overanalyze, chase meaning in things that don't matter, and by the time I realize it, I've already missed the moment God put right in front of me.

That's the tension. We say we follow Jesus, but we live chasing what's next. Planning, worrying, trying to control what we can't. We call it responsibility, but sometimes it's just faithlessness. Because God doesn't guide "later." He guides now. He calls you to see your wife now, to lead your kids now, to live in the moment He already gave you.

I've tried simplifying life, cutting things down to focus on what matters. But even that can become another distraction if I'm not careful. The truth is simple: my future is shaped by what I do right now. And what matters most is the Kingdom of God in my home. Not somewhere else. Not someday. Right here, in my living room, in my conversations, in how I show up.

When I get stuck in my head, I stop leading from my heart. My family feels it. The distance shows up. And the peace Jesus promised gets buried under the noise I created. That's where this hits hard. We don't just miss the moment, we push past what Jesus is already doing. We choose worry over trust, pressure over presence.

So the call is simple. Be present. See what God has already placed in your hands. You don't need more strategy or more time. You need clarity and obedience in this moment. This is your family. This is your calling. Do not miss it by living somewhere else.

Shepherding Value

Be Present in the Present — God's Kingdom is already in your home. Step into it with faith, courage, and presence.

Reflect

1. When your mind is racing—are you trusting Jesus or feeding anxious thoughts?

2. That distraction pulling you away—what is it costing you in your leadership at home?

3. In this moment with your family—how can you lead with presence instead of pressure?

Live It Today

Take intentional time today to sit with your family without distraction and fully engage with them.

Personal Prayer

Lord, quiet my mind and help me lead from presence, trusting You in this moment.

Reflective Verse

Matthew 6:34 (ESV)
"Therefore do not be anxious about tomorrow, for tomorrow will be anxious for itself…"

Day 71

You Might Lose Everything

2 Timothy 4:16–17 (ESV)
"At my first defense no one came to stand by me, but all deserted me. May it not be charged against them. But the Lord stood by me and strengthened me, so that through me the message might be fully proclaimed and all the Gentiles might hear it."

Some of you know exactly what this feels like. You used to run with people who felt like your circle, your support, your identity. But once you turned toward Christ, things shifted. Calls stopped. Conversations faded. You felt the distance grow, and somewhere in that silence, the question crept in, was it worth it? I've been there. Walking away from comfort, approval, and the image I built cost more than I expected. But it also revealed what was real.

Following Jesus strips things down. It exposes what you were holding onto, pride, control, and the need to be accepted. I had to let those go. Not once, but daily. That process is not clean or easy. It feels like loss at first. Relationships change. Some disappear. But what replaces them is different. Not larger circles, but stronger ones. Men who walk in truth. Men who hold the line. And in my own home, that strength grew deeper through walking in the Spirit with my wife.

The real risk is not losing people. The real risk is refusing to surrender. Because the things you protect, your comfort, your image, your habits, are the very things holding you back from leading. You cannot carry both. You cannot hold onto self and fully follow Christ. That is where the decision happens. Daily. Choosing to decrease so He can increase.

This is where leadership is forged. Not in comfort, but in cost. Not in approval, but in obedience. If you want to lead your home, it starts here. Laying down what you want so you can step into what God calls you to do. That means moving forward even when it feels like you are walking alone. Because you are not. The same truth Paul lived is still true, you may stand without others, but you will not stand without God.

You might lose something in this process. But what you gain is greater clarity, strength, purpose, and the presence of God. That is the trade. And it is worth it. Step forward. Take the risk. Lead with boldness, not because it is easy, but because it is right.

Shepherding Value

Faithful Boldness — A shepherd leader moves forward in obedience, trusting God more than comfort or approval.

Reflect

1. When relationships shift because of your faith—are you holding on or trusting God with the outcome?

2. That thing you are protecting—what is it costing you in your walk with Christ?

3. In your leadership at home—where do you need to choose obedience even if it costs you something?

Live It Today

Take one step today that reflects obedience to God over comfort or approval.

Personal Prayer

Lord, give me the courage to surrender what holds me back and lead with boldness in Your strength.

Reflective Verse

John 3:30 (ESV)
"He must increase, but I must decrease."

Day 72

Stand Up or Step Aside

Acts 4:13 (ESV)
"Now when they saw the boldness of Peter and John, and perceived that they were uneducated, common men, they were astonished. And they recognized that they had been with Jesus."

God's been calling, and too many men have been ignoring it. Not rejecting it, just delaying it. That was my story. I heard His voice when I was young, and I did nothing. Life moved forward, and I moved with it, chasing success, chasing control, drifting further from the very call I once heard clearly. Decades passed, but one thing didn't change: God never stopped calling.

Looking back now, it's clear how much I misunderstood. What felt like ambition was often pride. What looked like strength was fear. I lost things along the way, money, businesses, relationships. For a time, I almost lost my family. But through every loss, God was present. He didn't remove every consequence, but He never walked away. He guided, corrected, and protected me even when I wasn't paying attention.

Some men turn bitter in those moments. They blame God for the fire. I didn't. I saw Him as the only steady thing in the middle of it. Not a fallback plan, but the only true anchor. The fire didn't destroy everything, it refined it. Like gold under heat, the impurities surfaced and burned away. What remained was real. That process is not easy, but it is necessary.

Regret is real. Wasted time is real. But so is redemption. The call is still there. And now the focus is simple, stop drifting and start leading. Not perfectly, but faithfully. Not someday, but now. Because leadership starts in the home. Your wife sees it. Your kids feel it. And if Christ is not visible in you, they will not see Him clearly anywhere else.

This is what it means to stand up. Not to perform, but to follow. Not to impress, but to be present with Jesus. That is what marked Peter and John. Not education. Not status. Presence. Time with Christ. That is what changes a man, and that is what others will recognize.

Shepherding Value

Obedience over comfort — A shepherd responds when God calls, regardless of timing or difficulty.

Reflect

1. Looking back, where have you delayed acting on something God made clear?

2. What has that delay cost you in your leadership at home?

3. Right now, what is one area where obedience is required instead of more thinking?

Live It Today

Act on one clear area of obedience today without delay.

Personal Prayer

Father, remove my excuses and give me the strength to respond when You call.

Reflective Verse

Matthew 5:14 (ESV)
"You are the light of the world. A city set on a hill cannot be hidden."

Day 73

Back to the Big Picture

Luke 10:20 (ESV)
"Nevertheless, do not rejoice in this, that the spirits are subject to you, but rejoice that your names are written in heaven."

There was a season when I got so focused on being a great dad and a great husband that I completely missed the point. I thought if I could just do more, show up better, be stronger, or even be more "spiritual," that somehow my home would fall into place. But the more I tried to fix things in my own strength, the more anxious I became, and that anxiety drove me to clamp down harder on everything around me.

It didn't take long before that pressure turned into frustration, and frustration turned into distraction. I found myself overwhelmed, short-tempered, and missing what actually mattered. I was so locked in on performance that I lost sight of His presence. I was trying to lead from control instead of surrender, and in doing that, I lost the big picture of what God was doing in my home.

When we fixate on one part of the story, especially when that part is us, we drift from God's story. We begin to love and disciple from a place of insecurity instead of obedience. That's not leadership rooted in Christ. That's fear dressed up as effort. The question is not whether you're doing enough, but whether you are walking in step with the Spirit and keeping your eyes on Jesus.

Discipleship begins when we step back and recognize that we are not the savior of our homes. Jesus is. Our role is not to control outcomes but to point our families to Him through how we live, how we respond, and how we surrender. When we stop striving to prove ourselves and start yielding to God, everything shifts. That's where real leadership begins.

Shepherding Value

Leading from God's presence, not personal performance.

Reflect

1. You were trying to fix everything in your own strength—are you actually walking in step with Jesus or trying to prove yourself?

2. You became overwhelmed and anxious from pressure—what is driving your need to control instead of surrender?

3. You lost sight of the bigger picture at home—how is your leadership affecting your wife and children right now?

Live It Today

Pause today and intentionally release one area of control to God, choosing obedience over outcome.

Personal Prayer

Father, pull me out of performance and back into Your presence so I can lead the way You intended.

Reflective Verse

John 15:5 (ESV)
"Whoever abides in me and I in him, he it is that bears much fruit, for apart from me you can do nothing."

Day 74

Feel Nothing? Lead Anyway!

2 Timothy 4:2 (ESV)
"Preach the word; be ready in season and out of season; reprove, rebuke, and exhort, with complete patience and teaching."

There are days when everything feels right. You wake up ready, focused, and strong, and leading your home feels natural. You move with clarity, speak with purpose, and step into your role without hesitation. But then there are the grind days, the ones where everything feels flat. Your body is tired, your prayers feel empty, and the last thing you want to do is lead anything at all.

That's where most men drift. Not in rebellion, but in quiet passivity. You start waiting for something to change, your energy, your mood, your motivation. You tell yourself you'll step up when you feel it again. But while you wait, your wife and children are watching. They're not measuring your emotions. They're watching your consistency, learning what faith looks like by how you show up when nothing inside you wants to.

Paul told Timothy to be ready in and out of season. That means when you're on fire and when you're numb. When your home feels warm and when it feels cold. When respect is present and when it's not. Biblical manhood is not built on emotional highs. It's built on obedience in the ordinary, choosing to lead even when it feels like nothing is moving.

I've had seasons where I was just coasting. Not backsliding, not rebelling, just going through the motions. It wasn't some obvious failure that exposed me. It was comfort. It was waiting to feel inspired instead of choosing to obey. And that's when it hit me, my kids aren't waiting for an inspired father. They're watching for a faithful one who leads anyway.

Shepherding Value

Consistency — A faithful man leads with steady steps, even when the emotions are gone. Consistency is what builds trust, reveals character, and anchors a family in God's truth.

Reflect

1. You are waiting to feel strong before leading—are you obeying Jesus or waiting for emotion to lead you?

2. You have drifted into passivity during the grind—what comfort are you choosing over obedience right now?

3. Your family is watching your daily pattern—what are your wife and children learning from how you show up?

Live It Today

Lead one area of your home today with intentional obedience, even when you feel nothing.

Personal Prayer

Father, give me the strength to lead even when I don't feel strong. Help me stay faithful to You and to my family, especially when no one is watching.

Reflective Verse

Galatians 6:9 (ESV)
"And let us not grow weary of doing good, for in due season we will reap, if we do not give up."

Day 75

Sin Kills Character

Proverbs 4:23 (ESV)
"Keep your heart with all vigilance, for from it flow the springs of life."

I told God I was surrendered. More than once. The first time I said it, I meant it, or at least I thought I did. I had just been saved, and I gave Him my words. I told Him He could have my life, and He began to clean house. It wasn't instant. It took time, years of tearing down and rebuilding, and I believed I was all in. Fully surrendered.

But later, I saw it clearly. I had only given Him part of me. There was still hidden sin, still areas I controlled, still places where I called the shots while dressing it up in spiritual language. And again, I prayed it: "Lord, I'm totally surrendered." Now here I am again, seeing even more clearly. I wasn't surrendered then, and if I'm honest, there are still corners of my life I haven't fully handed over. But right now, with what I know, I say it again, and this time I understand what it costs.

The condition of the heart is everything. Jesus made it clear that what flows out of a man reveals what's inside. If your heart is carrying pride, laziness, bitterness, or hidden sin, it poisons everything downstream, your leadership, your words, your tone, your example. Sin doesn't sit quietly. It corrodes. It weakens your character like rust on steel and dulls the edge of your sword.

This is where men get it wrong. Surrender is not perfection. It's obedience. It's not about having strength or knowledge. It's about giving control back to God and choosing to live under His authority. Your family doesn't need a perfect man. They need a surrendered one. A man whose life reflects that his heart belongs to Jesus, not to himself.

Shepherding Value

Surrendered Obedience — True servant leadership begins when we lay down our own control and lead our families with a heart fully given to Jesus.

Reflect

1. You said you were surrendered—are you actually yielding your heart to Jesus or holding control in hidden areas?

2. You still carry pride or hidden sin—what is quietly shaping your character right now?

3. Your leadership flows from your heart—how is your current condition affecting your wife and children?

Live It Today

Confess one hidden area of your heart to God today and take one step of obedience to surrender it.

Personal Prayer

God, search my heart. I surrender every hidden place to You. Make me the man my family needs by shaping me into the man You want.

Reflective Verse

Psalm 51:10 (ESV)
"Create in me a clean heart, O God, and renew a right spirit within me."

Day 76

Your Broken 'Yes'

Matthew 5:37 (ESV)
"Let what you say be simply 'Yes' or 'No'; anything more than this comes from evil."

I didn't make promises lightly as a dad. When I said yes, I made sure nothing stood in the way of keeping it. Not time, not money, not mood, not convenience. If something could interfere, I didn't promise. I would say, "We'll see," or "Let me think on that." But I refused to throw out empty words, because my kids were listening then, and they're still listening now.

My word had to mean something. If I told my kids I would show up, I showed up. If I told my wife we would do something together, I followed through. Not because I'm perfect, but because I carry the name of Jesus, and He doesn't lie or overpromise. But there were times I failed. Times I had to look my family in the eye and say, "I was wrong," or "I didn't follow through." I didn't hide it. I owned it, because my family needed honesty more than a fake version of strength.

We live in a world full of noise and empty words. Men talk big but fail small at home. That's not leadership. That's lip service. Real leadership is built on integrity, quiet, steady, and unshakable. Jesus said to let your yes be yes and your no be no. That's not just about speech; it's about a life that matches your words. Every time your words don't match your actions, you weaken trust and teach your family that your leadership is unreliable.

This goes deeper than promises to your family. It reaches your yes to God. When you gave your life to Jesus, you said yes to obedience, surrender, and a new life. That yes is not a one-time moment. It's a daily decision. So slow down before you speak. Say yes when you mean it. Say no when you must. But whatever you say, live it. That's how a man leads his home with truth and reflects Christ.

Shepherding Value

Integrity — Integrity strengthens your role as a shepherd leader by anchoring your family in trust, stability, and truth.

Reflect

1. You have spoken promises before—are your words aligned with how you follow Jesus daily?

2. You have failed to follow through at times—what is keeping your words from matching your actions right now?

3. Your family depends on your consistency—how is your current pattern affecting their trust in your leadership?

Live It Today

Follow through on one commitment you have already made, or honestly correct one you have neglected.

Personal Prayer

Lord, help me to be a man who means what he says. Keep my words few, my heart steady, and my actions strong.

Reflective Verse

Ecclesiastes 5:5 (ESV)
"It is better that you should not vow than that you should vow and not pay."

Day 77

Your Broken 'Yes'

Matthew 5:37 (ESV)
"Let what you say be simply 'Yes' or 'No'; anything more than this comes from evil."

I didn't make promises lightly as a dad. When I said yes, I made sure nothing stood between me and keeping it. Not time, not money, not mood, not convenience. If something could get in the way, I didn't promise. I would say, "We'll see," or "Let me think on that." But I refused to throw out empty words, because my kids were listening, and they still are.

My word was and still is my bond. It had to mean something. If I told my kids I would show up, I showed up. If I told my wife we would do something together, I followed through. Not because I'm perfect, but because I carry the name of Jesus, and Jesus doesn't lie, flinch, or overpromise. But there were times I failed. Times I had to admit, "I was wrong," or "I didn't follow through." I didn't hide it. I owned it, because my family needed honesty more than a polished version of me.

We live in a world full of words and short on truth. Men talk big but fail small at home. That's not leadership. That's lip service. Real leadership is integrity, quiet, steady, and unshakable. Jesus said to let your yes be yes and your no be no. That's not just speech; it's a life that aligns with truth. Every time your words don't match your actions, you weaken trust and teach your family your leadership can't be depended on.

This goes deeper than promises to your family. It reaches your yes to God. When you gave your life to Jesus, you said yes to obedience, surrender, and laying down your pride. That yes is not a moment; it's a daily decision. So slow down before you speak. Say yes when you mean it. Say no when you must. But whatever you say, live it. That is how a man leads with integrity and reflects Christ in his home.

Shepherding Value

Integrity — Integrity strengthens your role as a shepherd leader by anchoring your family in trust, stability, and truth.

Reflect

1. You said yes before God—are you living in daily obedience to Jesus or drifting from that commitment?

2. You have spoken words that didn't match your actions—what is keeping your heart from full alignment right now?

3. Your family is learning from your consistency—how is your current pattern shaping their trust in your leadership?

Live It Today

Follow through on one commitment today or clearly correct one you have neglected.

Personal Prayer

Lord, help me to be a man who means what he says. Keep my words few, my heart steady, and my actions strong.

Reflective Verse

Ecclesiastes 5:5 (ESV)
"It is better that you should not vow than that you should vow and not pay."

Day 78

Get Off the Couch

James 1:22 (ESV)
"But be doers of the word, and not hearers only, deceiving yourselves."

Most men don't set out to fail their families. We say things with good intentions, but life crowds in. You plan to be home early, but work stretches longer. You promise time together, but exhaustion wins. You say you'll show up, but your attention drifts somewhere else. You didn't mean to break your word, but to your wife and kids, it still lands the same. It still feels like you chose something else over them.

I've stopped making promises I can't keep. Not because I care less, but because I care more. Instead of throwing out words, I want to live in a way that over-delivers. I want to go the second mile like Jesus called us to. Not just meeting expectations, but stepping beyond them. That means choosing obedience when it's inconvenient, choosing presence when it's easier to check out, and choosing sacrifice when comfort is calling your name.

There are always obstacles between your intention and your follow-through. Distractions, fatigue, pressure, old habits, they all stack up. You make a decision to lead, but each step between that decision and the outcome becomes a place where you can drift. That's why obedience isn't passive. It's deliberate. You don't wait for the right moment. You act because Christ is King, not because circumstances are easy.

I've had to face this in my own life. It's easy to talk about leadership, but much harder to live it out when you're tired or stretched thin. That's where the shift happens. Not in the big declarations, but in the quiet decision to stop coasting and start carrying the weight of what God has called you to. That means stepping up when you want to shut down and choosing to lead when everything in you says sit back.

Shepherding Value

Obedient Abandonment — Abandoning comfort for Christ leads to true strength and influence as a shepherd leader in your home.

Reflect

1. You hear the Word but delay obedience—are you actually following Jesus or just agreeing with Him?

2. You allow comfort and distraction to take over—what is pulling you away from intentional obedience right now?

3. Your family depends on your leadership—where are you choosing to coast instead of stepping up for them?

Live It Today

Choose one moment today to go beyond what is expected at home and lead with intentional obedience.

Personal Prayer

Lord, break my passivity and fill me with obedient strength. Help me abandon my comfort and lead my family with bold love and truth.

Reflective Verse

Luke 9:23 (ESV)
"And he said to all, 'If anyone would come after me, let him deny himself and take up his cross daily and follow me.'"

Day 79

Surprised By Jesus

Matthew 18:3 (ESV)
"And said, 'Truly, I say to you, unless you turn and become like children, you will never enter the kingdom of heaven.'"

Men, life will never go exactly as planned, and that's a gift whether you realize it or not. You weren't made to map out every detail or control every outcome. You were made to wake up with your eyes open and your heart ready, saying, "Father, lead me today." But most of us don't live that way. We grip our plans, chase certainty, and demand that life unfold on our terms, and in doing that, we miss what God is already doing right in front of us.

I've lived that tension. I used to hold tight to what I thought I knew. I needed everything to make sense, needed clarity, proof, and a path I could control. But the more I tried to control my walk with God, the more I suffocated it. I wasn't walking in faith, I was managing a system. And that system kept the focus on me instead of on Him.

The shift came when I started letting go, not just once, but daily. That's when I began to see it. The small moments, the unexpected provision, the people who showed up at the right time, the doors that opened when I was ready to quit. That's Jesus. He moves in ways we can't predict, but only when we make room for Him to move. Holding onto control blinds you. Surrender opens your eyes.

So stop clinging to your plan. Stop building your leadership, your fatherhood, and your home on your own understanding. That ground is unstable. Build it on trust. Wake up like a son who knows his Father is good, walk like a man who knows his steps are not his own, and lead like someone who follows Jesus first. That's not weakness. That's the strongest place a man can stand.

Shepherding Value

Wonder — When you lead your family with a sense of wonder in God, you help them see Him not as an idea to manage, but as a Father to trust.

Reflect

1. You try to control your path—are you trusting Jesus daily or managing your own plan?

2. You hold tight to certainty—what fear is keeping you from surrendering control right now?

3. Your family watches how you trust God—how is your current approach shaping their view of Him?

Live It Today

Release one area of control today and intentionally ask God to lead you in it.

Personal Prayer

Father, help me let go of control. I want to follow You today with childlike trust, ready for whatever You have planned.

Reflective Verse

Proverbs 3:5 (ESV)
"Trust in the Lord with all your heart, and do not lean on your own understanding."

From MenOfTheShepherd.com
Surprised By Jesus | June 1, 2025

Day 80

Your Secret Service

Matthew 6:1 (ESV)
"Beware of practicing your righteousness before other people in order to be seen by them, for then you will have no reward from your Father who is in heaven."

Men, leadership doesn't begin in the spotlight. It begins in the quiet. In the early hours, in the unseen decisions, in the small moments where no one is watching but God. That's where real strength is formed. Too many men are waiting for someone else to lead while their homes drift. Waiting has become normal. Pride has become hidden. And the enemy is taking advantage of both.

This morning I didn't jump out of bed. I laid there longer than usual, and the Lord pressed something deeper into me. Not about performance, but about pride. I've seen it in churches, groups, and ministries, and I've had to face it in myself. Even when we serve, there's that quiet pull, wanting to be noticed, wanting recognition. But the moment we chase the spotlight, we move away from the cross.

Jesus didn't serve for applause. He served in secret. He washed feet, not reputations. And when we crave the approval of others, it chokes out the Spirit's leading. That's the tension we have to face. Pride says, "Look at what I'm doing." Humility says, "God, do Your work in me." One path leads to burnout. The other leads to power rooted in Christ.

We are in a fight whether we acknowledge it or not. Our homes are under pressure, and our families are watching what we model as strength. If we lead with pride, they learn performance. If we lead with quiet obedience, they learn truth. That's the shift. Not louder leadership, but deeper surrender. Not visible success, but faithful obedience when no one sees.

Shepherding Value

Hidden Obedience — Leading as a man of God means doing the right thing even when no one is watching, trusting that God sees and honors what man never will.

Reflect

1. You serve but desire recognition—are you seeking Jesus or the approval of others?

2. You feel the pull of pride in your actions—what is driving your need to be seen right now?

3. Your family is watching your example—what are you teaching them about real leadership through your unseen choices?

Live It Today

Choose one act of servant leadership today that no one will notice but God.

Personal Prayer

God, help me silence my pride and follow Your lead. Teach me to serve when no one sees, and lead my family with quiet, steady faith.

Reflective Verse

Colossians 3:23 (ESV)
"Whatever you do, work heartily, as for the Lord and not for men."

Day 81

Quiet Cool, Silent-Strength

Matthew 6:1 (ESV)
"Beware of practicing your righteousness before other people in order to be seen by them, for then you will have no reward from your Father who is in heaven."

If you're a husband or a father, you're already leading someone. The real question is where you're leading them. It's easy to make noise about faith in public, to say the right things, to look the part. But leadership is not built on what people see. It's built on what happens when no one is watching. That's where the real condition of your heart is exposed.

This morning, in a quiet moment, it hit me, pride. Not loud, obvious pride, but subtle, creeping pride hiding under good Christian activity. I talk about servant leadership and shepherding, but I had to face the truth that there are times I care more about how my faith looks than whether I'm actually walking with Jesus. That tension is real, and if it's not confronted, it quietly erodes everything.

You can pray out loud and still neglect private prayer. You can teach your kids Scripture and still ignore your own time in the Word. You can say you trust God while trying to control everything. That's not leadership. That's performance. Jesus warned us about this because He knew how easily men would trade obedience for appearance. And when righteousness becomes a show, it loses its power.

The strongest men don't perform in front of others. They kneel when no one sees. They choose obedience in the quiet, reject temptation in the dark, and serve their families without recognition. That's where strength is forged. That's where a man becomes someone his family can trust to lead them toward Christ, not toward himself.

Shepherding Value

Quiet Obedience — Quiet obedience strengthens your role as a shepherd leader because it trains your heart to serve without needing applause. It sharpens your character in the dark so you can lead with light in the home.

Reflect

1. You speak about faith publicly—are you actually walking with Jesus in private obedience?

2. You care about how your faith appears—what pride is shaping your heart behind the scenes?

3. Your family follows your example—what are they learning from how you live when no one is watching?

Live It Today

Spend intentional time with God today in private, choosing obedience without recognition.

Personal Prayer

Lord, search my heart and show me where I've traded obedience for performance. I don't want to be loud for You and quiet in sin. I want to walk in truth, even when no one sees.

Reflective Verse

1 Samuel 16:7 (ESV)
"For the Lord sees not as man sees: man looks on the outward appearance, but the Lord looks on the heart."

Day 82

Lead Without Permission

1 Corinthians 15:58 (ESV)
"Therefore, my beloved brothers, be steadfast, immovable, always abounding in the work of the Lord, knowing that in the Lord your labor is not in vain."

When I first gave my life to Christ, I was on fire. That fire was real, and it drove me to pursue Scripture, to serve, and to lead. But what I found when I stepped into the church wasn't encouragement. It was hesitation, distance, and doubt. I was new, but ready. And instead of being guided, I was overlooked. When life hit hard and I needed support, the same place I ran to didn't know what to do with me.

That experience forced me to face something deeper. I was looking for validation from men instead of anchoring myself in what God had already spoken. I thought leadership required recognition, approval, or a title. But the truth is, calling doesn't come from people. It comes from God. And if He has called you, then waiting for permission becomes disobedience.

It took time to see it clearly. Years of growth, failure, and quiet learning. I had to let go of the need to be noticed and step into obedience without applause. I had to accept that my value didn't come from a platform, but from Christ. And in that place, God began shaping something deeper, something real. Not a performer, but a shepherd.

If you're waiting for someone to tell you you're ready, you've already missed it. You are called now. Leadership in your home doesn't begin with recognition. It begins with action. It's in the early mornings, the quiet prayers, the consistent presence, and the willingness to lead even when no one affirms it. Stop waiting. Step up. God already said go.

Shepherding Value

Spiritual Boldness — A man who walks in spiritual boldness doesn't wait for approval, he acts in obedience. This strength anchors the home and keeps the family rooted in God's Word.

Reflect

1. You are waiting for approval—are you obeying Jesus now or delaying what He has already called you to do?

2. You seek validation from others—what fear is keeping you from stepping forward in obedience?

3. Your family needs leadership today—where are you holding back instead of leading boldly at home?

Live It Today

Take one step today to lead your family spiritually without seeking recognition or approval.

Personal Prayer

Father, I don't need the world's approval. I want to lead my family the way You called me to. Remind me that in You, I am already enough.

Reflective Verse

Galatians 1:10 (ESV)
"For am I now seeking the approval of man, or of God? Or am I trying to please man? If I were still trying to please man, I would not be a servant of Christ."

Day 83

Break The Chains! Now!

Matthew 6:24 (ESV)
"No one can serve two masters, for either he will hate the one and love the other, or he will be devoted to the one and despise the other. You cannot serve God and money."

It started with good intentions. I was helping my family through a difficult season, and I don't regret that. But what followed was something I didn't see clearly at first. The pull to fix everything with more debt, better terms, lower payments, and longer timelines looked responsible on the surface. It gave the appearance of control, of stability, even of wisdom. But underneath all of it was something deeper, comfort, fear, and a desire to escape pressure instead of confront it.

I gave myself time to think, to weigh the options, to run the numbers. But in that waiting, God exposed what was really going on. This wasn't about finances. It was about trust. I had to face the reality that I was leaning on my own plans instead of depending fully on Him. What I called provision was actually control. What I called wisdom was covering fear. And that debt wasn't just a tool, it had become a chain.

That realization hit hard. Because once I saw it, I couldn't ignore it. Debt wasn't the only issue. It was just one form of a deeper problem, anything that pulls your focus away from Jesus has the power to enslave you. Whether it's money, comfort, pride, or addiction, the result is the same. It weakens your leadership, clouds your thinking, and keeps your heart from walking freely with God. That's not management. That's bondage.

So I made a different decision. A harder one. I chose discipline over comfort. I committed to attacking the problem instead of extending it. And with every step of obedience, something changed. Not just externally, but internally. As I let go of control and leaned into surrender, I felt closer to Christ. Not because of the outcome, but because of the obedience. That's where freedom begins.

Shepherding Value

Freedom through Discipline — Every choice to confront sin and fight for purity unlocks greater freedom to lead your family with power, purpose, and peace.

Reflect

1. You are trying to serve God while holding onto something else—what is competing with your devotion to Jesus right now?

2. You are justifying patterns that control you—what fear or comfort is keeping you from confronting it?

3. Your family depends on your clarity and strength—how is your current struggle affecting your leadership at home?

Live It Today

Identify one area of bondage and take a concrete step today to confront it with discipline and surrender.

Personal Prayer

Lord, I don't want to be mastered by anything but You. Help me kill the sin that keeps me distracted, and give me the strength to lead my home with a pure heart and a focused mind.

Reflective Verse

John 8:36 (ESV)
"So if the Son sets you free, you will be free indeed."

Day 84

No More Excuses

Matthew 6:33 (ESV)
"But seek first the kingdom of God and his righteousness, and all these things will be added to you."

I've been there. Broke, ashamed, and stripped down after a divorce I didn't see coming. No job, no food, and no desire to ask for help. Pride told me to hold it together. Shame told me to stay quiet. But neither of those voices were from God. They kept me stuck, trying to control what I clearly couldn't fix. And the longer I held onto that control, the further I drifted from the only place I needed to be, on my knees.

There was a Thanksgiving morning I will never forget. I had nothing in the house. Not even a can in the cupboard. And it was my turn to have the kids. I didn't have a plan. I didn't have a solution. But God did. That morning, someone showed up at my door with bags of groceries and a full turkey. I didn't earn it. I couldn't plan it. I couldn't control it. But God provided exactly what was needed, right on time.

That moment exposed something deeper. I thought strength meant holding everything together. But real strength is surrender. It's letting go of pride, admitting you don't have it, and trusting the One who does. Jesus didn't offer a suggestion when He said to seek first the kingdom. He gave a command with a promise. And when we ignore that, we don't just struggle, we lead our families into that same struggle.

Your family doesn't need a man pretending to have it all together. They need a shepherd who trusts God openly, prays boldly, and leads with obedience. If pride keeps you silent in your home, then pride is leading, not Christ. And if you keep waiting until you feel ready, you'll never step into what God already called you to do. The shift happens when you stop making excuses and start surrendering everything to Him.

Shepherding Value

Trust in God's Provision — A shepherd leader doesn't hoard control, he surrenders it, believing God will meet every need in His perfect timing.

Reflect

1. You say you trust God—are you actually seeking Him first or still trying to control your outcomes?

2. You hold onto pride and self-reliance—what is keeping you from fully surrendering right now?

3. Your family watches how you trust God—how is your current example shaping their faith at home?

Live It Today

Pray out loud over your family today and intentionally surrender one area you've been trying to control.

Personal Prayer

God, break down every wall of pride and fear in me. I surrender my control and ask You to teach me to lead with bold, steady trust in Your goodness.

Reflective Verse

Philippians 4:19 (ESV)
"And my God will supply every need of yours according to his riches in glory in Christ Jesus."

Day 85

Kill the Hero Inside

2 Corinthians 12:9 (ESV)
"But he said to me, 'My grace is sufficient for you, for my power is made perfect in weakness.' Therefore I will boast all the more gladly of my weaknesses, so that the power of Christ may rest upon me."

There was a season where I prayed almost every day, asking Jesus to help me focus on Him and to show me how to love Him through serving others. I wanted to lead well, to be obedient, to get it right. But I was frustrated. I had the desire, but no direction. I wasn't seeing results, and I kept telling myself to be patient. Underneath it all, though, there was something deeper I didn't want to face, I still wanted control.

That's where it hit me. My desire to serve wasn't always about Jesus. Sometimes it was about me, about feeling useful, respected, or strong. And the moment that became the motivation, I stepped back into the center of the story. That's the tension every man faces. We want to lead well, but we want to do it in our own strength. We want to be dependable, respected, and in control, even when we call it service.

But the truth is, the Spirit doesn't move through your strength. It moves through your surrender. When things don't go your way, when your leadership isn't recognized, when you feel stuck or overlooked, that's the moment of exposure. Are you serving Jesus, or are you serving your own expectations of what leadership should look like? If Jesus isn't the focus, then you are.

The shift comes when you stop trying to be the hero. When you admit your weakness, your need, and your limits, and let Christ lead through you. That's not failure, that's power. Your family doesn't need a man pretending to be strong. They need a man who points them to the only One who is. Real leadership begins when you step aside and let Jesus take His place at the center.

Shepherding Value

Dependence on Christ — When we lead from our weakness instead of our pride, we invite the power of the Holy Spirit to shape us into the shepherds our families need.

Reflect

1. You are trying to serve and lead—are you depending on Jesus or relying on your own strength?

2. You want control and results—what is revealing your struggle to surrender fully right now?

3. Your family looks to your example—how are you showing them dependence on Christ in your leadership?

Live It Today

Confess one area of self-reliance to God today and intentionally surrender it in prayer.

Personal Prayer

Lord, kill every part of me that still believes I can lead without You. Remind me that my strength is found in surrender, and teach me to lead with Your power, not mine.

Reflective Verse

2 Corinthians 12:10 (ESV)
"For the sake of Christ, then, I am content with weaknesses, insults, hardships, persecutions, and calamities. For when I am weak, then I am strong."

Day 86

Pluck the Plank

Matthew 7:5 (ESV)
"You hypocrite, first take the log out of your own eye, and then you will see clearly to take the speck out of your brother's eye."

Most of us don't need more teaching. We need to deal with the pride we've been carrying for years. Pride that convinces us we're right. Pride that makes it easier to judge than to forgive. Pride that hides behind leadership but is really just control. I know that because I lived it. I was wronged by people I trusted. Accused, misunderstood, and left without apology. And when I saw the same behavior in them later, everything in me wanted to prove I had been right all along.

That's when Jesus stopped me. Not gently, but directly. "Pluck the plank." Not theirs. Mine. I had spent days replaying conversations, carrying the sting, and holding onto the weight of it all. I wanted peace, but what I really wanted was justice. And instead of giving me what I wanted, God exposed what I needed, freedom from pride. The pain was real, but so was the pride growing around it.

It forced me to look inward instead of outward. To recognize the pain, name the pride, and take responsibility for my own response. That doesn't excuse what was done, but it reveals what was happening inside me. I couldn't lead anyone while carrying bitterness. I couldn't shepherd my family while holding onto judgment. That weight doesn't produce clarity. It produces blindness.

So I made a decision. Not to wait for an apology, not to demand resolution, but to forgive. To return to the altar and let God deal with them while He dealt with me. It's not easy. It doesn't feel fair. But it's the only path that leads to clean hands and a clear heart. And that's the kind of man my family needs to follow.

Shepherding Value

Forgiveness with Courage — This strengthens your role as a shepherd leader by freeing you to lead without hidden bitterness, showing your family the power of grace and the authority of Jesus over pride.

Reflect

1. You have been wronged—are you following Jesus in forgiveness or holding onto judgment?

2. You feel justified in your pain—what pride is shaping your response right now?

3. Your family sees how you handle conflict—what are you teaching them through your reaction?

Live It Today

Forgive someone today without waiting for acknowledgment and bring that situation before God in prayer.

Personal Prayer

Jesus, give me the courage to forgive where I want to prove a point. Help me lead my family with clean hands, not a bitter heart.

Reflective Verse

Romans 12:18 (ESV)
"If possible, so far as it depends on you, live peaceably with all."

Day 87

Be The Brick

1 Corinthians 3:11 (ESV)
"For no one can lay a foundation other than that which is laid, which is Jesus Christ."

For years I wrestled with what it meant not to cast pearls before pigs. I wanted to teach, correct, and help people grow, but I kept running into resistance. Hardened hearts, no hunger, no movement. It was frustrating. It made me question whether I was wasting time or missing something. But as I sat with that tension, God began to turn the focus back on me. Not on what others were doing, but on what was happening inside my own heart.

That's where the conviction hit. I thought others were the issue, but pride was the real problem. I wanted control. I wanted clarity. I wanted to decide who should lead and how things should be done. But Scripture made it clear that authority isn't mine to assign. God places people where He chooses. And that forced me to face something I didn't want to admit, I wasn't trying to be faithful, I was trying to be in charge.

That realization shifted everything. I am not the builder. I am not the one designing the structure. Jesus is the foundation, and my role is not to control the outcome but to submit to His placement. That means laying down my preferences, my expectations, and my need to be seen. It means trusting that where He puts me is exactly where I need to be, even if I don't understand it.

Being a brick means surrender. It means staying steady, reliable, and obedient in whatever role God assigns. Not fighting for position, not chasing recognition, but simply being available to be used. That's the kind of man my family needs. Not one who demands control, but one who trusts the Builder completely and allows his life to be placed on the foundation of Christ.

Shepherding Value

Obedience — True leadership starts when a man surrenders his plans and trusts God to place him where he's most needed in the Kingdom.

Reflect

1. You want to control outcomes—are you trusting Jesus as the foundation or trying to build your own way?

2. You resist your current role—what pride is keeping you from surrendering to where God has placed you?

3. Your family depends on your steadiness—how are you showing them obedience in your daily life?

Live It Today

Accept your current role today and serve faithfully in it without seeking recognition or control.

Personal Prayer

God, I lay down my pride. Place me where You want me, and give me the strength to stay there. I want to be used for Your Kingdom, not my comfort.

Reflective Verse

Romans 13:1 (ESV)
"Let every person be subject to the governing authorities. For there is no authority except from God, and those that exist have been instituted by God."

Day 88

Leave the Altar

Luke 10:27 (ESV)
"And he answered, 'You shall love the Lord your God with all your heart and with all your soul and with all your strength and with all your mind, and your neighbor as yourself.'"

Jesus made it simple. Love God. Love others. But if I'm honest, loving God often feels easier than loving people when it costs something. I can show up, read the Word, and feel like I'm doing the right things. But when it comes to stepping into tension, owning my part, or making something right, that's where I hesitate. And that hesitation isn't harmless. It's disobedience dressed up as delay.

I've had moments where I knew exactly what needed to be done. A conversation I didn't want to have. A wrong I needed to make right. And instead of moving, I stayed at the altar. I told myself I was praying, thinking, waiting for the right time. But the truth was, I was avoiding discomfort. I was holding onto pride. Jesus didn't leave room for that. He said if you remember someone has something against you, you stop, leave, and go. Not later. Not when it feels easier. Now.

That's the turning point. The altar feels safe, but obedience often takes you away from that place and into something uncomfortable. And I've had to learn that I don't step into that alone. When I finally moved, when I stopped delaying and chose obedience, Jesus met me there. He gave me the words, the humility, and the strength I didn't have sitting still. What I thought would break me actually freed me.

So I've had to face it, if I stay at the altar while ignoring what God has already told me to do, my worship becomes noise. Real leadership isn't just prayer. It's action. It's stepping into the hard moments, making things right, and leading my family from a place of obedience instead of comfort. That's where real change happens.

Shepherding Value

Courageous Obedience — This strengthens your role as a shepherd leader by proving that faith isn't just something you believe, it's something you obey—even when it costs you comfort.

Reflect

1. You know what Jesus has asked of you—are you obeying Him now or delaying what He already made clear?

2. You hesitate in difficult moments—what pride or fear is keeping you from acting right now?

3. Your family is watching your response—how are you modeling obedience when it costs you something?

Live It Today

Take immediate action on one conversation or step of obedience you have been avoiding.

Personal Prayer

Father, give me the strength to leave the altar and do what You've already told me to do. I don't want to delay any longer.

Reflective Verse

Matthew 5:24 (ESV)
"Leave your gift there before the altar and go. First be reconciled to your brother, and then come and offer your gift."

Day 89

Lead With Grit, Not Silence

Matthew 7:12 (ESV)
"So whatever you wish that others would do to you, do also to them, for this is the Law and the Prophets."

It's easy to measure manhood by what we avoid. Don't cheat, don't lie, don't mess up. I lived there for a while, thinking that staying quiet and out of trouble made me a good man. But that standard is weak. It keeps you passive. It keeps you comfortable. And it keeps your leadership from actually building anything that lasts. Avoiding sin is not the same as pursuing what is right.

The shift came when I started seeing what Jesus actually modeled. He didn't just avoid wrong, He actively did good, even when it cost Him. That forced me to look at my own life. I could say the right things, believe the right things, and still be doing very little to lead my home with intention. That's where passivity hides. It convinces you that doing nothing wrong is enough, when in reality your silence is leaving a gap your family needs you to fill.

I had to confront that. My home needed more than a man who stayed out of trouble. It needed a man who acted. Who showed love, not just spoke it. Who stepped in when it was uncomfortable. Who chose presence over distraction and sacrifice over ease. That's where real leadership shows up, in the daily decisions that cost something and reflect Christ to the people closest to you.

When I started leaning into that, it changed the way I saw everything. My wife isn't just someone I live with, she's my first neighbor. My kids aren't just responsibilities, they're disciples watching every move I make. And they don't learn from what I avoid. They learn from what I pursue. That's where grit replaces silence, and leadership becomes visible instead of assumed.

Shepherding Value

Proactive Goodness — Proactive goodness strengthens your role as a shepherd leader by turning passive protection into active spiritual influence, both inside and outside your home.

Reflect

1. You avoid obvious sin—are you actively following Jesus by doing good in your daily life?

2. You stay comfortable and quiet—what is keeping you from stepping into intentional action right now?

3. Your family watches your example—how are you showing them what pursuing good actually looks like?

Live It Today

Do one intentional act today that reflects Christ's love in your home without being prompted.

Personal Prayer

Lord, help me reject passivity and pursue the good You've called me to do. Fill me with Your grace so my wife and kids see You in my actions, not just my words.

Reflective Verse

James 4:17 (ESV)
"So whoever knows the right thing to do and fails to do it, for him it is sin."

Day 90

Lead and Shepherd or Fall and Die!

1 Corinthians 16:13 (ESV)
"Be watchful, stand firm in the faith, act like men, be strong."

As men of the Shepherd, surrendered to Jesus and called to lead our homes, we face more than everyday pressure. There is a real battle for our families, and it doesn't come in obvious ways. It shows up in distraction, passivity, and a slow drift away from intentional leadership. I've seen it in my own life, showing up physically but not leading spiritually, thinking presence was enough when direction was missing. That gap is where everything starts to weaken.

The truth is, the enemy isn't just after you. He's after your home, your marriage, your children, and what comes after you. And if we don't take that seriously, we hand it over without a fight. I had to confront that reality. Being around my family wasn't the same as shepherding them. Providing wasn't the same as leading. And if I didn't step up with purpose, my silence was shaping the direction more than I realized.

That's where the shift had to happen. Leadership means setting the tone, not just reacting to it. It means opening the Word, praying out loud, speaking truth, and creating rhythms that point your family to Christ. Not because it feels natural, but because it's necessary. I've had to choose that intentionally, choosing to lead when I felt tired, to speak when it would be easier to stay quiet, and to guide instead of drift.

It's not easy. It's consistent, gritty obedience. But it's also where strength is built. When you step into that role, your home begins to anchor itself differently. Not around comfort or routine, but around Christ. And that's the responsibility we carry. Not to manage a household, but to shepherd it with conviction and clarity.

Shepherding Value

Bold Spiritual Initiative — Men who take spiritual initiative don't wait for perfect timing. They lead with courage, model obedience, and shape the spiritual atmosphere of their home.

Reflect

1. You are present in your home—are you actively leading your family in obedience to Jesus or just existing alongside them?

2. You feel the pull of distraction and passivity—what is keeping you from stepping into intentional leadership right now?

3. Your family follows your direction—how are you shaping their spiritual life through your daily actions?

Live It Today

Lead one intentional moment today by opening Scripture or praying out loud with your family.

Personal Prayer

Father, give me the courage to lead and the clarity to hear Your voice. I don't want to blend in. I want to stand firm and lead my family with bold faith.

Reflective Verse

Joshua 24:15 (ESV)
"And if it is evil in your eyes to serve the Lord, choose this day whom you will serve… But as for me and my house, we will serve the Lord."

Day 91

Lead Your Home Like a Man

Ephesians 5:23 (ESV)
"For the husband is the head of the wife even as Christ is the head of the church, his body, and is himself its Savior."

Every man knows when he's drifting. I've felt it. Showing up, working hard, paying the bills, but knowing something deeper was off. My home was running on autopilot, and I assumed that my effort would naturally translate into leadership. It didn't. When I wasn't intentional, my family didn't see a shepherd. They saw a man who believed in God but wasn't actively leading them toward Him.

I had to face that reality. Providing isn't the same as shepherding. Being present isn't the same as leading. When I left the spiritual direction of my home to chance, others filled the gap, culture, screens, and outside voices shaping what my kids believed. That wasn't what God called me to. He called me to lead, not just exist alongside my family.

The shift came when I started taking ownership. Not in big, dramatic moments, but in daily decisions. Opening the Bible at the table. Praying out loud over my wife. Asking my kids real questions about their hearts. Turning off distractions and stepping into conversations that mattered. It wasn't always easy, but it was necessary. Leadership started showing up in the small, consistent actions that pointed my family to Jesus.

This is what I've learned, headship is not about control. It's about responsibility. Christ didn't dominate the church; He died for it. That's the standard. Leading your home means laying down your comfort, your distractions, and your passivity. It means choosing to step up every day, even when it's inconvenient, and guiding your family toward Christ with clarity and conviction.

Shepherding Value

Ownership — Owning your role as the spiritual leader in your home gives your family the shepherd they need and points them to Christ.

Reflect

1. You feel the drift in your home—are you actively leading your family toward Jesus or letting others shape them?

2. You rely on effort alone—what is keeping you from taking full responsibility for your spiritual leadership?

3. Your family follows your example—how are your daily actions guiding them toward or away from Christ?

Live It Today

Lead one intentional moment today by opening Scripture or praying out loud with your family.

Personal Prayer

Lord, wake me up to the responsibility You have given me in my home. Teach me to lead with courage, to love with action, and to step into the role of shepherd for my family.

Reflective Verse

Deuteronomy 6:6–7 (ESV)
"And these words that I command you today shall be on your heart. You shall teach them diligently to your children, and shall talk of them when you sit in your house, and when you walk by the way, and when you lie down, and when you rise."

Day 92

Burnout, Balance, and the Man of the Shepherd

Mark 8:36 (ESV)
"For what does it profit a man to gain the whole world and forfeit his soul?"

Burnout doesn't usually hit all at once. I've learned it creeps in slowly, hidden behind good intentions and full schedules. You keep pushing, telling yourself it's just a busy season. But seasons stretch, and before you realize it, you're exhausted, short-tempered, distant from God, and giving your family whatever scraps are left. I've been there, working, serving, building, and still feeling like I was losing ground where it mattered most.

It took me time to see that more effort wasn't fixing anything. I was giving more but producing less. The harder I pushed, the more disconnected I became, from my wife, my kids, and my walk with God. And the truth hit me hard: this wasn't just fatigue. It was misalignment. I was saying yes to too many things that pulled me away from the very people God called me to shepherd. That's not leadership. That's drift.

I'm living this right now. Carrying work, ministry, projects, and responsibilities that kept stacking up until something had to give. Stress at home, pressure at church, and constant demands exposed how thin I had stretched myself. I could feel it breaking me down. And instead of pushing harder, I had to make a decision that didn't feel natural, to step back. Not from my family or my calling, but from everything else that was stealing strength from both.

That shift matters. Because you can't shepherd well when you're empty. Jesus stepped away to pray and reset, and I've had to follow that example. Stepping back is not quitting. It's realigning. It's choosing to invest in your family, to reconnect with God, and to lead from a place of strength instead of depletion. That's where clarity returns, and that's where real leadership begins again.

Shepherding Value

Intentional Reset — Stepping back from overload allows a shepherd leader to restore strength, refocus on God, and lead his family with clarity and purpose.

Reflect

1. You feel stretched and exhausted—are you aligning your life with Jesus or overloading yourself beyond His direction?

2. You keep pushing through fatigue—what is preventing you from stepping back and resetting right now?

3. Your family receives what is left—how is your current pace affecting your ability to lead them well?

Live It Today

Remove one unnecessary commitment today and replace that time with prayer or focused time with your family.

Personal Prayer

Lord, show me where I have taken on more than You asked of me. Help me step back, reset, and lead my family with strength, clarity, and peace.

Reflective Verse

Luke 5:16 (ESV)
"But he would withdraw to desolate places and pray."

Day 93

Truth, Legacy, and Courage: A Shepherd's Call in Uncertain Times

Ephesians 5:15–16 (ESV)
"Look carefully then how you walk, not as unwise but as wise, making the best use of the time, because the days are evil."

After stepping back for a season, I came back with clarity. Sometimes you have to get quiet long enough to hear what actually matters. And what I keep coming back to is this: the world doesn't need more noise. It needs men who lead with truth, urgency, and courage inside their homes. The pressure around us, cultural, social, spiritual, is real. But the call hasn't changed. Walk wisely. Use your time well. Lead your family with intention.

Truth has to come first. The world is loud, fast, and reactive. People rush to speak before they understand, to react before they reflect. But as men, we are responsible for slowing that down in our homes. Teaching our families to value truth means modeling restraint, asking better questions, and anchoring everything in God's Word. That kind of leadership protects your home from fear and confusion. It creates stability when everything outside feels unstable.

At the same time, moments like this remind you how fragile life really is. You don't control tomorrow. That reality forces a decision, either drift or lead with purpose. I've had to look at my own life and ask what actually lasts. Not schedules, not plans, not achievements. Legacy is built in daily conversations, in forgiveness, in showing your family what matters most. Small, intentional moments shape the long-term direction of your home.

And none of that happens without courage. Not loud, reactive courage, but steady, controlled leadership. Fear wants to set the tone. Division wants to enter your home. But you decide what atmosphere your family lives in. You decide whether your house reflects chaos or Christ. That means guarding your tone, your words, your reactions, and leading with love and self-control even when everything around you pushes the opposite direction.

Shepherding Value

Courageous Leadership — Leading with truth, urgency, and steady courage establishes a home grounded in Christ rather than shaken by culture.

Reflect

1. You are surrounded by noise and opinions—are you leading your family toward truth or reacting with the culture?

2. You know life is fragile—how are your daily actions shaping the legacy your family will carry forward?

3. You feel pressure and uncertainty—are you allowing fear to set the tone in your home or leading with courage and self-control?

Live It Today

Set aside ten minutes today to lead your family in truth—read Scripture, ask one honest question, and guide the tone of the conversation.

Personal Prayer

Father, give me wisdom to lead with truth, urgency to build a lasting legacy, and courage to guide my family with steady faith.

Reflective Verse

2 Timothy 1:7 (ESV)
"for God gave us a spirit not of fear but of power and love and self-control."

From MenOfTheShepherd.com
Truth, Legacy, and Courage: A Shepherd's Call in Uncertain Times | September 21, 2025

Day 94

Leading Without Rushing: A Shepherd's Call to Wait

Habakkuk 2:3 (ESV)
"For still the vision awaits its appointed time; it hastens to the end, it will not lie. If it seems slow, wait for it; it will surely come; it will not delay."

You ever get ahead of yourself? You think you know what God is doing, so you move fast, only to realize you moved without Him. I have been there. Missions in Thailand felt clear, urgent, and right. I researched, planned, and moved forward quickly. I was ready to sell my house and step into what I believed God had for me. But I was not actually following Him, I was following my own excitement. I rushed ahead, assuming clarity meant timing.

It took time to see the mistake. I lost money, lost time, and more importantly, I drifted from God in the process. I was moving so fast toward what I thought was His will that I stopped walking with Him. That was the real loss. It forced me to confront something deeper, trust is not proven in action alone, but in waiting. I had to look back and admit that movement is not always obedience.

This is where shepherding becomes real. You look ahead at your family and wonder what the future holds. Will your children follow God? Will your leadership produce something lasting? You want answers, direction, and certainty. But your role is not to control outcomes, it is to lead faithfully where you are. God handles the timing. A man who rushes creates confusion. A man who waits develops clarity.

If you are going to lead your family well, then you must learn from the past without living in it. Face where you moved too fast. Admit where urgency replaced obedience. Then step back under Christ's leadership and walk with God at His pace. Lead with patience. Trust that what He has spoken will come in its time.

Shepherding Value

Patience — A shepherd learns from past mistakes by refusing to rush ahead of Christ and leading his family at God's pace.

Reflect

1. You moved fast—where have you rushed ahead of Jesus instead of waiting for His direction?

2. You assumed clarity meant timing—what past decision exposed your impatience or need for control?

3. You created confusion by rushing—how can you lead your family with patience and steadiness now?

Live It Today

Identify one place where you rushed ahead before, and pray before taking any further action today.

Personal Prayer

Lord, slow me down where urgency has replaced obedience, and teach me to lead at Your pace.

Reflective Verse

Proverbs 3:5–6 (ESV)
"Trust in the LORD with all your heart, and do not lean on your own understanding. In all your ways acknowledge him, and he will make straight your paths."

Day 95

Pride Doesn't Listen

1 Kings 12:8 (ESV)
"But he abandoned the counsel that the old men gave him and took counsel with the young men who had grown up with him and stood before him."

Rehoboam didn't lack guidance. He rejected it. The counsel was clear, serve the people, lead with restraint, speak with wisdom. But it didn't match what he wanted, so he ignored it. He chose voices that supported his position instead of voices that challenged his heart. What followed wasn't just a bad decision, it was a divided kingdom.

I can look back and see seasons where I thought I was doing the Lord's work, but something underneath it was off. I wanted recognition. I wanted to know I was doing it right. I wanted to be seen as a man who leads well. And without realizing it, that desire started shaping my decisions more than obedience did. I didn't call it pride at the time. I called it responsibility. But it wasn't coming from surrender, it was coming from self.

The cost didn't show up immediately. It built slowly. Conversations that didn't land right. Tension that lingered longer than it should have. Moments where I should have listened, but I moved forward instead. What I thought was strength started creating strain. And I had to face it, this wasn't just a leadership issue. It was pride working underneath everything I was doing.

The turning point is owning it. Not explaining it away. Not softening it. Just admitting it. Pride creates division before you even realize it's there. And until you confront it, you'll keep leading from the same place. But when you do, something changes. You stop trying to prove yourself and start submitting yourself.

The shift is learning to lead from a different place. You slow down. You listen. You stop chasing recognition and start pursuing obedience. You allow Christ to shape how you lead instead of trying to control how you're seen. That's where healing begins. That's where trust starts to rebuild.

Shepherding Value

Humility — A shepherd lays down the need to be right and chooses to be shaped by Christ.

Reflect

1. You wanted to be seen as right—where has that desire shaped your leadership more than obedience to Christ?

2. You moved forward from self—what tension in your home reveals where pride has been at work?

3. You've seen the cost—what would it look like to lead from humility instead of needing recognition?

Live It Today

Choose one conversation today where you intentionally listen without needing to prove anything.

Personal Prayer

Lord, remove the need in me to be seen or proven right, and teach me to lead from humility under You.

Reflective Verse

James 4:6 (ESV)
"But he gives more grace. Therefore it says, 'God opposes the proud but gives grace to the humble.'"

Day 96

Lead What's In Front of You

Matthew 6:34 (ESV)
"Therefore do not be anxious about tomorrow, for tomorrow will be anxious for itself. Sufficient for the day is its own trouble."

I'm going to speak straight, brother to brother. You want to lead your home well. You love God. You want to be a steady husband and a present father. But you're tired, anxious, and carrying thoughts you were never meant to carry. I know that because I do it too. My wife tells me I think too much, and she's right. I overanalyze, chase meaning in things that don't matter, and then miss the moment God put right in front of me.

That's the tension. We say we follow Jesus, but we live chasing what's next. Planning, worrying, trying to control what we can't. We call it responsibility, but sometimes it's just faithlessness. God doesn't guide "later." He guides now. He calls you to see your wife now, to lead your kids now, to live in the moment He already gave you.

I've tried simplifying life, cutting things down to focus on what matters. But even that can become another distraction if I'm not careful. The truth is simple: my future is shaped by what I do right now. And what matters most is the Kingdom of God in my home. Right here, in my living room and conversations.

When I get stuck in my head, I stop leading from my heart. My family feels it. The distance shows up. And the peace Jesus promised gets buried under noise I created. That's where this hits hard. We don't just miss the moment, we push past what Jesus is already doing. We choose worry over trust, pressure over presence.

So the call is simple. Be present. See what God has already placed in your hands. You don't need more strategy or more time. You need clarity and obedience in this moment. This is your family. This is your calling. Do not miss it by living somewhere else.

Shepherding Value

Presence — A shepherd leads his family by obeying Christ in the moment God has already placed before him.

Reflect

1. You chase what's next—are you trusting Jesus now or feeding anxious thoughts about later?

2. You miss the moment God put right in front of you—what distraction is pulling your heart away from obedience today?

3. You stop leading from your heart—how is your family experiencing your pressure instead of your presence?

Live It Today

Give your full attention to one family conversation today without planning, fixing, or mentally leaving the moment.

Personal Prayer

Lord, pull my heart back into this moment and teach me to lead my family with presence, trust, and obedience.

Reflective Verse

Matthew 6:33 (ESV)
"But seek first the kingdom of God and his righteousness, and all these things will be added to you."

Day 97

You're Not Listening

James 1:19 (ESV)
"Know this, my beloved brothers: let every person be quick to hear, slow to speak, slow to anger."

You hear the words, but you're not really listening. You respond fast. You explain. You correct. You move the conversation where you want it to go. On the surface, it feels like leadership, clarity, direction, decisiveness. But underneath it, something is missing. You're not taking in what's actually being said.

I've done this more times than I want to admit. My wife is talking, and I'm already forming a response before she finishes. My kids are speaking, and I'm filtering what they're saying through what I think they should say. I hear them, but I'm not listening. And because of that, I miss what's really going on in their hearts.

The tension builds quietly. Conversations stay shallow. Frustration shows up in small ways. The people you're called to shepherd start holding things back, not because they don't care, but because they don't feel heard. And that lands on you. Not as failure, but as misalignment. You're leading, but you're not connected.

The turning point is realizing that listening is not passive, it's leadership. You stop trying to control the conversation. You stop rushing to respond. You let silence do its work. You actually hear what's being said without needing to fix it immediately. That's where understanding begins.

The shift is intentional. You slow down your words. You pay attention to tone, not just content. You make space for your family to be honest without interruption. And in doing that, you lead differently, not by controlling the outcome, but by engaging the heart. That's where trust grows. That's where real shepherding happens.

Shepherding Value

Listening — A shepherd leads by hearing the heart before trying to direct the outcome.

Reflect

1. You respond quickly—where are you speaking before you've fully listened?

2. You control the conversation—what are you missing because you're not hearing the heart behind the words?

3. You lead without connection—how would your leadership change if you slowed down and truly listened?

Live It Today

Have one conversation today where you listen fully without interrupting or preparing your response.

Personal Prayer

Lord, slow my words and open my ears so I can lead my family by truly listening.

Reflective Verse

Proverbs 18:13 (ESV)
"If one gives an answer before he hears, it is his folly and shame."

Day 98

You Don't Control What's Next

Proverbs 19:21 (ESV)
"Many are the plans in the mind of a man, but it is the purpose of the LORD that will stand."

You're trying to get ahead of it. Planning, thinking, adjusting, trying to make sure what's coming lands the way you want it to. It feels responsible. It feels like leadership. But underneath it, there's a pressure that doesn't come from God. It comes from needing to control what hasn't happened yet.

I've done this. Looking ahead, trying to line everything up, thinking if I just plan it right, I can avoid the struggle or guarantee the outcome. It sounds wise on the surface, but it slowly shifts from trust to control. And the more I try to control what's next, the less I actually walk with God in it.

The tension shows up when things don't go as planned. Frustration. Adjustment. More pressure. And if I'm not careful, I start forcing decisions instead of following direction. What I thought was leadership turns into me trying to make something happen that God hasn't actually released yet.

The turning point is recognizing that the future is not yours to control, it's yours to trust. God has already gone ahead of you. He doesn't need your pressure to fulfill His plan. He asks for obedience, not management. And when that lands, it exposes how much of your "planning" was really about control.

The shift is surrender. You still plan, but you hold it loosely. You still prepare, but you stay responsive. You stop forcing outcomes and start trusting God's timing. That's where peace returns. That's where direction becomes clear, not because you figured it out, but because you stayed aligned.

Shepherding Value

Trust — A shepherd releases control of outcomes and follows God's direction with confidence.

Reflect

1. You're trying to control what's next—where has planning turned into pressure in your life?

2. You force outcomes—what situation are you trying to make happen instead of trusting God's timing?

3. You feel the weight—what would it look like to release control and follow God's direction instead?

Live It Today

Identify one area where you're forcing an outcome and consciously release it to God today.

Personal Prayer

Lord, take control of what I've been trying to manage, and teach me to trust Your timing fully.

Reflective Verse

Ecclesiastes 3:11 (ESV)
"He has made everything beautiful in its time."

Day 99

What Are You Actually Trusting

Proverbs 3:5 (ESV)
"Trust in the LORD with all your heart, and do not lean on your own understanding."

You say you trust God. But your decisions tell the truth. When pressure builds, you default to what you can control. You calculate, adjust, and move based on what makes sense to you. It feels responsible. It feels wise. But if you're honest, a lot of it is still you leaning on yourself.

There have been moments where I paused, not because God said wait, but because I didn't have enough clarity to feel comfortable moving forward. I told myself it was wisdom. But looking back, it was hesitation. I wasn't waiting on God. I was waiting on certainty. And those are not the same thing.

The tension shows up when the future isn't clear. You feel it. That pull to take control, to secure something, to make sure you don't miss it. But that's the moment your trust is exposed. Not when things are steady, but when they're uncertain. What you do there reveals what you actually believe.

The turning point is honesty. You stop pretending your control is faith. You admit where you've been leaning on your own understanding. And you recognize that real trust doesn't wait for clarity, it moves in obedience even when the outcome isn't visible.

The shift is deliberate. You choose to trust God beyond what you can see. You make decisions based on His direction, not your comfort. You release the need to have everything figured out. And in that place, your leadership changes. It's no longer driven by fear of the future, but by confidence in the One who holds it.

Shepherding Value

Faith — A shepherd leads by trusting God's direction even when the future is unclear.

Reflect

1. You say you trust God—where are your decisions still controlled by what makes sense to you?

2. You hesitate without clarity—what situation is exposing your reliance on your own understanding?

3. You want certainty—what would it look like to act in obedience without needing to see the outcome?

Live It Today

Take one step of obedience today where you've been waiting for full clarity.

Personal Prayer

Lord, help me trust You beyond what I can see and lead with faith instead of control.

Reflective Verse

Hebrews 11:1 (ESV)
"Now faith is the assurance of things hoped for, the conviction of things not seen."

From MenOfTheShepherd.com
Faith Doesn't Wait for Clarity | May 6, 2025

Day 100

Now Go Lead Together

Hebrews 10:24–25 (ESV)
"And let us consider how to stir up one another to love and good works, not neglecting to meet together… but encouraging one another…"

You didn't go through this just to finish a book. You went through this to become a different man. A man who leads. A man who listens. A man who walks with Christ in his home. But if this stays with you alone, it will fade. That's the reality. Growth that isn't shared rarely lasts.

There's a reason God didn't design this to be done alone. Leadership sharpens in relationship. You see it, you hear it, you're challenged by it. And you need that. I've seen what happens when men try to carry this by themselves. It starts strong, but over time it drifts. Not because they don't care, but because they're alone.

This is where it changes. You take what you've learned and you bring other men into it. Not to impress them. Not to teach them like you've mastered it. But to walk it out together. That's where the weight of this actually sticks. That's where real growth happens.

The turning point is deciding this doesn't stop here. You move from personal growth to shared growth. You stop consuming and start engaging. You stop reading and start building. And it doesn't need to be complicated. It just needs to be consistent.

The shift is simple. Find two other men. Meet weekly. Talk honestly. Pray directly. Stay grounded in Scripture. No performance. No pretending. Just men who want to lead their homes better and follow Christ more closely. That's enough. That's where transformation happens.

Shepherding Value

Multiplication — A shepherd strengthens his leadership by walking with other men who pursue Christ together.

Reflect

1. You've grown through this—who are two men you can invite into this journey with you?

2. You tend to do this alone—what has that cost you in consistency and accountability?

3. You want to lead well—what would it look like to grow alongside other men instead of by yourself?

Live It Today

Reach out to two men and invite them to meet weekly—even if it's simple and informal.

Personal Prayer

Lord, give me the courage to step out of isolation and grow alongside other men who are pursuing You.

Reflective Verse

Ecclesiastes 4:9–10 (ESV)
"Two are better than one… For if they fall, one will lift up his fellow."

Build It With Other Men

This doesn't continue unless you take it beyond yourself.

Start simple. Don't overthink it.

Form a triad of three men.

- One where you are
- One ahead of you
- One behind you.

How to Meet:

Meet once a week for 30–60 minutes.

- Check in honestly (real life, not surface)
- Discuss one topic from life or this book
- Talk it out directly and honestly
- Pray briefly and specifically.

Keep It Strong:

No teaching mode; no fixing each other; no pretending; stay consistent.

Practical Setup:

Face-to-face if possible; if not, use phone, video, or app; meet at the same time each week; protect the time.

Final Charge:

You are responsible for what you've learned.

- Lead your home.
- Walk with Christ.
- Bring other men with you.

When Brotherhood Lacks Direction

Groups don't stay the same, and they're not supposed to. I've seen triads grow, shrink, split, and form again. That's not failure. That's growth. John 12:24 (ESV) says, "Truly, truly, I say to you, unless a grain of wheat falls into the earth and dies, it remains alone; but if it dies, it bears much fruit." Done right, groups don't just last, they multiply.

I was invited into a triad with men who did not know why they were meeting. There were different life stages, different family structures, and different priorities, but none of it had been addressed. There was confusion. No clarity. No direction. No purpose. Proverbs 29:18 (ESV) says, "Where there is no prophetic vision the people cast off restraint, but blessed is he who keeps the law." That is exactly what was missing.

What followed exposed everything. The conversation turned inward. Men talked about themselves instead of growing together. There were no guardrails, no humility, no shared mission. It did not sharpen anyone. It revealed pride.

The next week it got worse. Between meetings, I had publicly made the decision to pursue a leadership role in the church. When I returned, I was accused and called dishonest and disloyal because I had not come to them first. That expectation had never been stated. There was no agreement, no defined loyalty, and no shared process. What they expected was never established.

Here is the lesson. Brotherhood without clarity will collapse. A group without purpose will turn inward. Men without humility will create conflict instead of growth. Proverbs 16:3 (ESV) says, "Commit your work to the LORD, and your plans will be established." That includes how you build with other men.

So if you are going to do this, do it right. Define the purpose. Set clear expectations. Focus on growth, not performance. Stay grounded in humility. This is not about control or position. It is about becoming better men together under Christ.

My Personal Prayer To You

I pray as you move forward, and if you choose to share this with other men in your life, whether in your church, your family, or your community, that Jesus is always with you. I pray that you always make space for Him and continually seek Him as your Father, your brother, and your friend. God bless you.

Appendix: How to Use This Devotional

This devotional is designed to be simple, direct, and consistent. Use it daily or as part of a group. The goal is not perfection but steady growth as a man who leads under Christ.

Individual Use

You can read one day at a time, five days a week, or even one day a week as a simple reflection. Keep it consistent and honest. This is not about information, but about alignment, correction, and growth.

Additional encouragement and teaching are available through the Men of the Shepherd YouTube channel.

Search **@menoftheshepherd** on YouTube or visit **MenOfTheShepherd.com** for organized videos and resources.

Group Use (Men's Groups)

This devotional can be used in a simple weekly format. Read five days during the week and meet once a week with other men.

Share key takeaways, struggles, and insights. Keep discussion focused and honest, and encourage accountability, not performance. Do not overcomplicate it.

Men's groups do not need to be rigid. If your group moves faster or slower, that is fine. If you finish early or take longer, that is fine.

The goal is not to complete a schedule but to grow together. A simple 12-week rhythm can be helpful.

Weeks 1–11: read and meet weekly.

Week 12: review, reflect, and discuss growth and next steps.

For Leaders

If you are leading a men's group and want more support, a free resource is available. Visit **MenOfTheShepherd.com** to download the group guide and access additional resources.

MenOfTheShepherd.com

9 7 9 8 9 9 9 5 1 7 2 8 2 6